The short guide to social work

Robert Adams

First published in Great Britain in 2010 by

The Policy Press
University of Bristol
Fourth Floor
Beacon House
Queen's Road
Bristol BS8 1QU
UK

t: +44 (0)117 331 4054
f: +44 (0)117 331 4093
e: tpp-info@bristol.ac.uk
www.policypress.co.uk

North American office:
The Policy Press
c/o International Specialized Books Services
920 NE 58th Avenue, Suite 300
Portland, OR 97213-3786, USA
t: +1 503 287 3093
f: +1 503 280 8832
e: info@isbs.com

British Library Cataloguing in Publication Data
A catalogue record for this book is available from the British Library.

Library of Congress Cataloging-in-Publication Data
A catalog record for this book has been requested.

ISBN 978 1 84742 287 3 paperback

Cover design by The Policy Press
Cover photo: courtesy of www.alamy.com
Printed and bound in Great Britain by Hobbs, Southampton

Contents

List of tables and figures iv

List of abbreviations vi

A note on the terms used in this book ix

Introduction xi

Part 1: Preparing for social work

one Introducing social work 3

two Qualifying programmes in social work 31

three Becoming a social worker 47

four Organisation, legal basis and regulation of social work 65

Part 2: Practising social work

five Social work with children, young people and their families 89

six Social work with adults and health-related services 125

seven Social work with older people 149

eight Social work with disabled people 167

nine Social work with mental health, illness and recovery 183

ten Social work with groups and communities 203

Postscript 215

References and further reading 217

Appendix: Information about post-qualifying programme 231
    structures

Index 235

List of tables and figures

Tables

1.1	Main adult social care services	4
2.1	Stages of application for the qualifying social work programme	32
2.2	Direct and indirect knowledge and understanding	35
2.3	Evaluating the placement experience	40
2.4	General criteria for assessment of student's assignments	41
2.5	Values and principles of social work	43
2.6	National Occupational Standards for social work: a summary	44
4.1	Selected legislation related to social care and social work	78
5.1	Welfare checklist	97
6.1	Concepts and components in the process of contracting services	131
6.2	Personalisation and delivery of health and social care services	134
6.3	Illustrations of legal provisions relating to the rights of adults	136
6.4	Illustrations of legal provisions regarding rights to services	136
6.5	The four bands of needs	140
7.1	Relevant legal provisions	153
7.2	Checklist of areas forming the basis of dignity in work with older people	157
8.1	Illustrations of legal provision for services for disabled people	172
8.2	Models of disability	175
9.1	Models of mental health problems and responses to them	186
9.2	Social work roles and titles in mental health work	191

Figures

1.1	Themes of social work	8
1.2	Maslow's pyramid of needs	14
1.3	Roles of social workers	17
1.4	Continuum of social work practice	18
1.5	Social work intervention, creative and empowering work	26
2.1	What has been learned (spider chart)	38
2.2	Components of assessment criteria	40
3.1	Components of expertise	59
3.2	Ingredients of integrative activity	62
4.1	Family tree of the UK courts and tribunals	74
4.2	Multiple accountabilities of a social worker	79
5.1	Contrasting dimensions of childhood and views of children	93
5.2	Child-centred practice	103
6.1	Commissioning and coordinating adult social care services	134

7.1	Continuum of services for older people	155
9.1	Democratic team	192
9.2	Hierarchical team	192
9.3	Range of settings for delivery of mental health services	193
9.4	Sources of referrals of child and family to CAMHS	195
9.5	Approaches to practice	195
A.1	Proposed career structure of social workers	232

List of abbreviations

A&E	accident and emergency (department)
ADHD	attention-deficit hyperactivity disorder
AMHP	approved mental health practitioner
APL/APEL	accreditation of prior (experiential) learning
ASW	approved social worker
BASW	British Association of Social Workers
CAFCASS	Children and Family Court Advisory Support Service
CAMHS	child and adolescent mental health services
CAT	credit accumulation and transfer
CCW	Care Council for Wales
COP	code of practice
COS	Charity Organisation Society
CPPIH	Commission for Patient and Public Involvement in Health
CQC	Care Quality Commission
CRB	Criminal Records Bureau
CSCI	Commission for Social Care Inspection
CSSI	Care and Social Services Inspectorate Wales
CSV	Community Service Volunteers
DCSF	Department for Children, Schools and Families
DH	Department of Health
DHSS	Department for Health and Social Services
DHSSPS	Department of Health, Social Services and Public Safety
ECHR	European Convention on Human Rights
EU	European Union
FCWO	Family Court Welfare Service
GP	general practitioner (doctor)
GSCC	General Social Care Council
HCC	Healthcare Commission
HIW	Healthcare Inspectorate Wales
IASSW	International Association of Schools of Social Work
IFSW	International Federation of Social Workers
IT	information technology

LINks	local involvement networks
NAW	National Assembly for Wales
NHS	National Health Service
NISCC	Northern Ireland Social Care Council
NOS	National Occupational Standards
NTA	National Treatment Agency for Substance Misuse
PCT	primary care trust
PLO	practice learning opportunity
RQIA	Regulation and Quality Improvement Authority Northern Ireland
SCRC	Scottish Commission for the Regulation of Care
SEN	special educational needs
SfC	Skills for Care
SSC	Sector Skills Council
SSLP	Sure Start local programme
SSSC	Scottish Social Services Council
Topss	Training Organisation for the Personal Social Services
UCAS	Universities & Colleges Admissions Service
UNCRC	United Nations Convention on the Rights of the Child
WAG	Welsh Assembly Government

A note on the terms used in this book

Two striking illustrations of the reality that social work deals with problematic aspects of people's lives is the fact that social workers engage with the labels used to refer to people and sometimes to discriminate against them and exclude them from society.

What to call the people with whom we work?

There is no single term used throughout the UK, let alone throughout other western countries, for the person with whom social workers work. In settings where therapy or counselling is the main focus, the term 'client' tends to be used and sometimes social workers adopt this word. In healthcare settings, the term 'patient' may be used and adopted by social workers, for instance, in hospitals. In adult social care, 'service user' and 'carer' are used widely, or 'person who uses services'. Sometimes also, words such as 'customer' or 'consumer' are used in local government and public services. In advocacy work, terms such as 'service adviser', 'consultant' and 'expert through experience' are also used. Each of these words has supporters and critics. Throughout this book, the terms 'service user' and 'client' are used most often, depending on whether the focus of practice lies closer to social care or therapeutic work.

How to refer to people's physical or learning impairment or disability

In short, do we refer to 'disabled people' or 'people with a disability'? There is no simple answer to this, because social workers need to be prepared to work with people with physical and learning impairments in ways that do not reinforce any stigma they may experience. This is complex, in the sense that, traditionally, agencies have tended to treat people with impairments as different and, consequently, have contributed to devaluing them. Over the past half century, people with physical and learning impairments have campaigned against disablism – discrimination on the grounds of disability – and one of their main grounds has been that their identities should not be determined by their impairment but by impairment being a pretty well universal human experience.

Discrimination against disability is different from sexism and racism, in that a person who does not experience impairment today may do so in the future, which means that an able-bodied person who has tended to regard impaired people as different now may experience the negative identity brought about through becoming impaired. A further complication is that while some people with impairments regard being identified as in need of 'disability' services as stigmatising and objectionable, others do not object to what they regard as the reality that they are dependent on services and on other people.

The individual model of disability tends to focus on tackling the physical or the mental impairment purely as a characteristic of the person. The social model of disability distinguishes between that impairment and the social factors that contribute to that person being disabled, that is, regarded and treated as different and perhaps as less able than others.

This book recognises the complexity of these arguments. On the whole, the term 'disabled people' is used where it is appropriate to acknowledge the ways society disables people. On some occasions, terms such as 'child with a learning disability' may be used, where this seems more appropriate.

Introduction

Social work is a profession uniquely placed to help people. It helps individuals and families to meet their personal and social needs. It acts as a bridge between people and their social circumstances. It is *the* 'social' profession among the many professions that make up public services. It is concerned fundamentally with upholding principles of social justice and equality, ensuring that people receive their entitlements, their rights are protected, they are safeguarded from abuse, that vulnerable people are supported, that socially excluded people are included and that people are not discriminated against on the basis of age, gender, sexuality, disability, faith, culture, geography or any other difference.

Social work aims where possible to empower people to receive services personalised to meet their needs. It enables people who experience problems as they proceed through life to gain the confidence, understanding and resources they need in order to tackle these problems. Social workers engage not only with individuals but also with groups – including family groups – neighbourhoods and communities. They make connections between people's individual situations and social factors, so that they can achieve personal and social fulfilment.

Social work has survived several decades of political challenges from governments and social challenges from the mass media who have portrayed social workers as the villains in people's lives, without whom the world would be a happier place. While some of these ill-informed negative stereotypes of social workers persist, the social work profession has entered the 21st century stronger than ever before.

Qualification for practice as a social work professional in the UK is via an undergraduate degree in social work, which, as social work is since the 2000 Care Standards Act a protected title, is followed by entry to the Social Care Register (including social workers).

Social workers manage tensions between intervention and prevention, between intervening in people's lives and empowering them. Social work offers practitioners opportunities to work creatively with people at vulnerable points in their lives, empowering them by giving them access to expertise and resources. At the same time, social work presents challenges, since practitioners also exercise legal powers of intervention in the lives of individuals, families and communities, where problems require intervention, to safeguard children and adults by reducing or preventing harm.

Social work is a profession that draws on practitioners' personal qualities as well as on their knowledge, understanding and skills. It is important for social workers to be open and self-aware, receptive to new ideas as well as able to receive criticism. Becoming a social worker is an opportunity to continue with personal as well as professional development.

This book is a guide for new entrants to social work. Entry into the social work profession is a process of simultaneous engagement with oneself, as with the subject matter of other people's lives. The structure of the book is as follows.

Part 1 deals with preparing for entry into a qualifying programme for social work. It contains four chapters, each of which tackles one major aspect of this process. Chapter One introduces social work, by putting it in context and describing what it is about and what social workers do. Chapter Two discusses what qualifying programmes in social work consist of and what they require. Chapter Three takes one key aspect of becoming a social worker – clarifying our own biography and our journey into applying for the qualifying programme – and takes this apart. Chapter Four gives some idea of how social work is organised, what its legal basis is, how it relates to the legal system and, finally, how its standards of services are regulated and inspected.

Part 2 deals with six main areas of social work practice. Chapter Five looks at social work with children, young people and their families. Chapter Six tackles social work with adults and the closely related aspects of the health services. Chapter Seven explores social work with older people, Chapter Eight examines social work with disabled people and Chapter Nine discusses social work with people with mental ill health. The final chapter looks at group work and work with communities, and explores some of their common features as well as distinctive aspects. This is a suitable way to end the book, as it is a reminder of the breadth of social work practice, spanning work with individuals, groups and communities.

Part 1
Preparing for social work

1

introducing social work

Introduction

This chapter defines social work and puts it in its historical and social context. It then illustrates its key features, indicates how it meets people's needs and concludes by identifying what social workers do in practice.

What is social work?

Social work is a modern profession which forms part of a broad span of social care activities carried out by a huge workforce in the health and social care services. The repeated use of the word 'social' in this sentence indicates the need to clarify the meanings of these different 'socials'.

Wide array of social care services

Social security is the term often used to refer to the various monetary welfare benefits available for people, either universally as with retirement pensions, or means-tested as with 'meals on wheels' (meals brought to people's homes). **Social care** is the generic term used to refer to the personal social services provided directly or indirectly by local authorities (in the sense that alongside services directly provided, many services are indirectly provided, that is, commissioned by local authorities from private, voluntary and independent providers). **Social services** include a huge array of child and adult social care services for the person and for the carer, provided in the person's own home, through day services or in residential or nursing homes (see Table 1.1 for the main ones).

Table 1.1: Main adult social care services

Type of service	What it entails
Children and families	Social work services for families Family support Safeguarding children Under-fives services Childcare 'Looked-after' children, adoption, fostering Specialist services for children Disabled children Children with special educational needs (SEN) Youth services
Vulnerable adults	Services to protect adults at risk of, or experiencing, abuse
Hearing impairment and deafness	Services provided within the National Audiology Framework
Blindness and visual impairment	Services for partially sighted and blind people
Disability	Services for disabled people
Autism	Services for people with autistic spectrum disorder
Learning disabilities	Services for learning disabled people
Advocacy	A range of advocates for people and services to enable them to self-advocate
Mental health	Services for people with mental health problems
Mental capacity	Services under the 2005 Mental Capacity Act, to safeguard the rights of people who lack capacity
Housing	A range of housing provision to meet people's needs

The precise size of the social care workforce is unknown but an authoritative estimate (Eborall, 2005, pp 1-2) gives the total as 922,000 people, 1.6 million if extra support staff in education and health services are included, 61% of whom are working with older people, 19% with disabled adults, 13% with children and 7% with people with mental ill health.

This total is less than 10% of the healthcare workforce, which increased from 1,071,562 (including 701,324 qualified clinical staff) in 1998 to 1,368,693 (including 529,731 qualified clinical staff) in 2008 (see NHS Staff 1998-2008 Master Table, www.ic.nhs.uk/statistics-and-data-collections/workforce/nhs-staff-numbers/nhs-staff-1998--2008-overview).

Nature of social work

Social work is a single profession, but under this general heading a great variety of practice exists. Cree (2003, p 3) acknowledges that it is not possible to make a simple statement about what social work means to all practitioners, clients and people who use services. Within the UK, there are different emphases between practitioners, within different geographical areas – urban and rural, well-off and less well-off, industrial and non-industrialised – and between the approaches favoured by different practitioners. Social workers with UK qualifications and registration by the professional bodies of the four different countries of the UK (General Social Care Council [GSCC] [England], Northern Ireland Social Care Council [NISCC], Scottish Social Services Council [SSSC] and Care Council for Wales [CCW]) are recognised increasingly in different countries.

Social work has different international identities in different continents and countries. Nevertheless, social work academics and practitioners recognise the advantages of developing a global presence for the range of practices under the general umbrella of 'social work'. Accordingly, the International Federation of Social Workers (IFSW) and the International Association of Schools of Social Work (IASSW) jointly define social work as follows:

> The social work profession promotes social change, problem solving in human relationships and the empowerment and liberation of people to enhance well-being. Utilising theories of human behaviour and social systems, social work intervenes at the points where people interact with their environments. Principles of human rights and social justice are fundamental to social work. (IFSW, 2000)

Social work is very much about bringing about change in people's lives as individuals, in families and in communities. It has the capacity to bring about social change as well, through enabling policy makers and politicians to reframe personal and social problems. As governments in many countries recognise the complexity of problems encountered by people, individually, in families, in social groups and in the community, social work as a profession is developing in order to tackle these problems. It is important to understand that in the UK, as in many other parts of the world, social work originates in the growing understanding that much can be done to help vulnerable individuals and families to cope with the more demanding and complex problems of living, between one extreme of expecting them to help themselves (traditional self-help) and the other extreme of shutting them away in institutions (orphanages, children's homes, institutions for people with physical impairments or learning disabilities, mental hospitals, old people's homes and so on).

How did social work originate?

From the late 18th century, in the US and western European countries including the UK, there was a general move towards confining poor, disabled, mentally ill and criminal people in institutions, sometimes for many years, or even the rest of their natural lives. Between the late 18th and early 19th centuries, criminals were increasingly executed or transported to penal colonies in Australia.

Many of the activities associated with modern social work in the UK can be traced back to somewhat more philanthropic initiatives in the second half of the 19th century. The foundations of social work recognisable in the 20th century lie in the model of individual casework developed by the Society for Organising Charitable Relief and Repressing Mendicity (that is, begging), generally known as the Charity Organisation Society (COS), founded in London in 1869, whose members were usually women in the respectable middle classes (Stedman Jones, 1971, p 256), who aimed to encourage self-help and inculcate God-fearing respectability among families who had fallen on hard times. The COS caseworkers did not waste their efforts on those considered to have sunk so far into pauperism or depravity that they were incapable of helping themselves. Like the guardians of the 1834 Poor Law Amendment Act, they drew a sharp distinction between those considered 'deserving' and 'undeserving'. They rewarded and reinforced the Victorian values of hard work, self-help, respectability and thrift.

More broadly, the different components of modern social work can be traced to a number of diverse and sometimes interconnecting historical movements and traditions. Entire books have been written about small parts of each of these, but to summarise some of the most important, these include:

- Ideas about the causation and treatment of problems of the human mind: psychoanalytic theories developed by Siegmund Freud (1856-1939) from the late 19th to the early 20th centuries became part of a rich and diverse field of theories, approaches and social work methods.
- Psychological and sociological, leading to psychosocial approaches to social work.
- Behavioural and cognitive psychologies, leading to cognitive behavioural therapies.
- Mutual aid: Friendly Societies originated in much older associations between people, often involving regular saving and pooling this money as insurance to tide people over hard times, such as sickness, unemployment and funeral expenses.
- Working people's education organisations: these were set up from the early 19th century to advance knowledge, understanding and help personal advancement in work and the community.
- Community development: this was action, exemplified in the Toynbee Hall settlement in East London in the late 19th century, to develop improved housing and a more hygienic and healthier urban environment.
- Utopian communities: provision of all-in-one communities from Robert Owen in New Lanark in the early 19th century to such entrepreneurs and social pioneers as Seebohm Rowntree in New Earswick, York, the Cadbury family in Bourneville, Birmingham, James Reckitt in Hull and Titus Salt in Saltaire near Bradford.

Nature of present-day social work

We can make a link between these many influences and three facets of modern social work, organised around three key themes: individual treatment or therapy; self-help; and mutual aid and community development (see Figure 1.1).

Figure 1.1: Themes of social work

Individual treatment

Psychoanalytic ideas

Therapeutic intervention

Psychosocial casework

Cognitive behavioural

Self-help and independence

Self-improvement and hard work

Penitence and restitution

Reform and spiritual growth

Themes of social work

Mutual aid
Community development
Community action and community work

Modern social work still embraces these three themes identified above, although in the 21st century these go under different labels, such as individual or personalised treatment, self-education and training and citizen participation and empowerment. In brief, social work is about the three distinctive but linked areas of professionals doing things to people, people doing things for themselves and people doing things together and with the community. Social work performs the functions of enabling people, individually, in families, groups and communities to deal with the complexity of personal and social problems which otherwise would threaten their chances of enjoying satisfying and fulfilled lives. The breadth of social work contributes to its uniqueness as a profession. Social workers carry out work with children and their families, as well as with adults.

Social work can be regarded as the leading social profession. **Social** is the word used to refer to people's relationships with other people, including families and the community. The social aspects of social work draw on research and understanding from sociology and social policy – a societal collective rather than individual focus. Sociological insights result from research and critical commentary, for instance, on the impact on people's lives of social inequalities such as poverty, poor housing, prolonged unemployment and lack of equal access to educational, sporting and leisure facilities, sometimes referred to as social exclusion. **Social exclusion** is the general term used to refer to the different ways in which some people are unable to gain access to social roles and community, educational and leisure activities with other people.

World, European and UK-based social work

Although social work is well established as a profession in many industrialised parts of the world, its character varies in different countries. Although in Australia and New Zealand, for instance, social work is very similar to UK social work, in many countries that were formerly part of the Union of Soviet Socialist Republics (USSR), for instance, the notion of community-based social work support is still developing, to replace the traditional reliance on residential institutions. Children with physical impairments or learning disabilities, for example, were often institutionalised, supported by ideas and assumptions such as 'defectology' (what Lubovsky, 1974, at the Institute of Defectology in Moscow, refers to as 'the science of handicapped children'). In some of these countries, social work is a relatively young profession. In Uzbekistan, in 2009, out of a population of about 27 million there were fewer than 200 social workers; some had been formally trained through university, others were retrained former workers from residential institutions that had been closed down. Much of the effort in such countries is devoted to expanding the provision of resources to support people in the community, where often, without social work support, many disabled, mentally ill and vulnerable children and adults would have been placed in these institutions, once existing medical and social supports in the community were exhausted.

Workforce of UK social workers

In the UK there are about 79,500 registered social workers and about 15,900 student social workers, about three quarters of whom are employed by local authorities, in line with the English survey by Eborall, which found that in 2003-04 about 78% of social workers in England were employed by local authorities (Eborall, 2005, p 2). About three quarters of the social workers in the UK are women and half work part time. Just under half work in children's services, just over half the remainder working in specialist, including health, settings and just under half in adult services. Social workers make up about 7.5% of the total social care workforce.

Key features of social work

Four main features give social work its prominence and contribute to its lead position as a social profession:

1. Social work draws on wider environmental (that is, family, group, community and societal) understandings of people's circumstances than those that are merely personal, that is, located in the individual.
2. Social work is rooted not just in psychology and human development, but also in all the social sciences, such as sociology, philosophy, political science and anthropology.
3. Social work advocates for perspectives on people's lives and problems that engage with the consequences for them of persistent inequalities, discrimination, stigmatisation and social exclusion.
4. Social work is very largely a statutory profession. That is, social workers act on behalf of the state, exercising legal duties and powers in carrying out their responsibilities: to safeguard, protect and support people, empower them and enable them to manage their problems. In some circumstances, social workers intervene compulsorily in people's lives, to prevent people harming themselves or others.

These four components of the 'social' in social work are in constant friction with each other. This gives social work its critical character, its position at the heart of uncertainty in people's lives and its potential to engage with personal and social change.

Position of social work in society

Because social work deals with people's problems and often has to exercise the responsibilities of the state towards family members – sometimes protecting one family member from another – it tends to be intrinsically linked with controversy. Its subject matter can be important, life-changing decisions affecting the interests of one family member against those of another. For instance, an abused child, or the child of a heroin-addicted lone parent, may have to be looked after by the local authority on an emergency basis and subsequently adopted.

Unsurprisingly, therefore, the professionalism of social workers has at its core the requirement that they not only work well with people but have the capacity to understand people's lives holistically in all their complexity and reach sound recommendations and decisions when necessary.

Social work, therefore, is a very rewarding profession because it engages with people's lives often at times when they face changes, crises and problems; but for these very reasons social work is also a demanding profession. Social work also occupies an ambiguous place in society. From time to time, the decisions made by local authorities and professionals in social work attract controversy.

Family situations are often complex and there are no ready solutions to many problems people face in their lives. There tend to be different options, with advantages and disadvantages attached to each. Also, the future is inherently uncertain and it is often impossible to predict what will happen. Social work therefore takes place in conditions of human and social uncertainty.

Currently, practitioners are expected to display

■ an adherence to the research basis for practice;
■ an informed scepticism;
■ confidence to challenge prevailing statements within families where necessary, so as to protect those family members – whether older, disabled or with mental ill health, single parents or children – who are vulnerable.

We should take these measures as positive indications of the importance of social work and the vital necessity for the quality of services to be sustained. These are signs that the crucial role of social work is being recognised by government and that the profession is gaining in prominence in society. There are five main reasons for this:

■ the professional status of social work has achieved a higher profile;
■ the workforce of social workers has expanded significantly;
■ since the 1990s, a degree-level basic qualification in social work has been introduced;
■ the introduction of a structured programme of post-qualifying education for social workers has contributed to the enhanced importance of continuing professional development;
■ the growing importance of evidence-based practice in social work has been enhanced by the growing body of qualitative and quantitative social work research.

Social work and meeting people's needs

What is meant by need?

At the most basic level (Adams, 2008a), there is clarity about what people need in order to survive, in terms of food, shelter and nurturing. At the upper levels of need, there would probably be little argument that people also need satisfaction from living fulfilled and happy lives. However, between these extremes, and in terms of how to describe and respond to these basic needs, there is much scope for debate. Maslow (1908-70) developed a much quoted hierarchy of needs in the early 1940s (Maslow, 1943), based on a five-level pyramid, from basic physical 'deficiency' needs to the higher and more personally fulfilling 'growth' needs, the assumption being that the satisfaction of lower levels enables the person to move on to higher levels. However, and what is very useful from the point of view of clarifying the full scope of social work, Maslow added three more levels of 'growth' needs in the 1960s, not usually included in the diagram of his pyramid of needs, but making a more complete statement of human needs (see Figure 1.2). What we gain from this is an holistic picture of people's needs.

Needs are relative, not absolute

However, a person's needs are not a fixed fact that can be assessed by the professional and responded to. The nature and intensity of a person's needs is not absolute, but varies according to the setting – it is relative to time and place. Modern notions of poverty distinguish **absolute poverty** (conceived and measured according to a fixed level of wants) from **relative poverty** (a constantly reconstructed level, changing in keeping with dominant expectations and living standards). The level at which a person was just about lifted from poverty, for instance, in Victorian Britain was significantly lower than it is in the 21st century. We take for granted now that most people will live in houses with a mains power supply with ready access to basic sanitation and running water. Also, needs appear differently depending on the vantage point from which they are viewed. Bradshaw (1972) identifies four types of social need:

- *normative need*, which is assessed according to a predetermined norm;
- *comparative need*, which is expressed in terms of what other people need;
- *experienced need*, which is how people experience what they need rather than how others assess it;
- *expressed need*, which is stated by people on the basis of personal experience.

In short, not only are people's needs relative, they are a social construct, and the way we refer to them depends very much on our focus.

Figure 1.2: Maslow's pyramid of needs

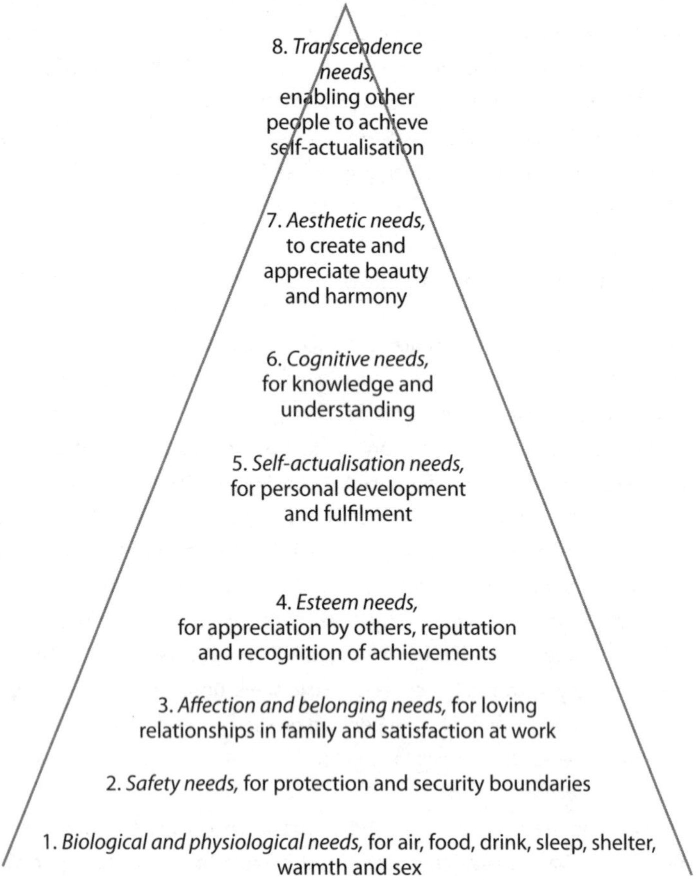

8. *Transcendence needs,* enabling other people to achieve self-actualisation

7. *Aesthetic needs,* to create and appreciate beauty and harmony

6. *Cognitive needs,* for knowledge and understanding

5. *Self-actualisation needs,* for personal development and fulfilment

4. *Esteem needs,* for appreciation by others, reputation and recognition of achievements

3. *Affection and belonging needs,* for loving relationships in family and satisfaction at work

2. *Safety needs,* for protection and security boundaries

1. *Biological and physiological needs,* for air, food, drink, sleep, shelter, warmth and sex

Holistic approaches to meeting people's needs

Social work in the UK commonly adopts an holistic approach to meeting people's needs. The word 'holistic' came into the above discussion of Maslow's conception of needs. In this setting it refers to meeting the needs of the whole person in their family, social and community setting. We can see how this fits with government policy since 2000, by reference to services for adults, children and families:

- *Services for adults:* the government set out a strategy in 2007 for the development of health and social care services for people (DH, 2006), and for an approach providing them with more choice and independence (HM Government, 2007). The development of integrated services (integrated in the sense that a range of health and social services work collaboratively towards common goals, using shared approaches) in areas such as mental health services, palliative care (holistic care to meet the needs and maximise the quality of life of people with advanced, often progressive conditions and illnesses), end-of-life care and disability (see Chapters Six to Nine).
- *Services for children and families:* the range of integrated health, education and social services developed under the general government policy banner of Every Child Matters, aiming among other things to promote the health and well-being of children. *The Children's Plan* (DCSF, 2008) is a 10-year plan aiming to improve services for children and young people (see Chapter Five).

Needs and rights

There is a tension between needs and rights, as noted earlier in this chapter. Social workers commonly act to challenge or prevent discrimination, to promote equality of treatment and to preserve people's rights. A useful approach to understanding and meeting people's needs, to which many social workers can relate, is to base social work with people on notions of human rights. The 1948 United Nations (UN) *Universal Declaration of Human Rights* states that all people have fundamental rights and freedoms, regardless of differences between them, such as their birth, 'race' or age, irrespective of their age, 'race', birth or other differences. The 1990 UN Convention on the Rights of the Child (UNCRC) asserts that the rights and needs of children of any age take priority over those of adults. (Incidentally, the Welsh Assembly has adopted this Convention but the Westminster Parliament has not.) Another way to understand this is to state that children are more vulnerable than adults to their basic needs not being met and their rights not being upheld. We find, therefore, the basic principle of the 1989 Children Act – a cornerstone of current social work with children and families – being that where any decisions about a child and their family are being made by professionals, the welfare of the child rather than their rights must be regarded as paramount (see Chapter Five for more discussion of this).

People meeting their own needs: direct payments and personalisation

The 21st century has witnessed a general movement towards greater choice in local services for individuals and families who are vulnerable or otherwise in need. Personalisation reforms have been implemented in England between 2008 and 2011. Personalisation originates partly in the social work values of client self-determination and respect for people (Carr, 2008, p 8), and partly in the broader government agenda for modernisation of the public sector, set in motion in 1997 and updated in a progress report a decade later (PMSU, 2007). Two central principles of this are

- empowering citizens to shape their own lives;
- tailoring services to citizens' needs and wishes.

It was applied to adult social care in a parallel government publication (HM Government, 2007), which introduced to social work and social care the two principles central to personalisation:

- enabling people to choose the services they need;
- ensuring people could exercise control over their services.

Personalisation is not without its critics, and there are three main types of criticism:

- that giving people choice is a disguised way of the state shedding responsibility for their welfare, which can still be regulated by setting overall budgets and controlling the criteria determining who is eligible for services;
- that it is managerially demanding, potentially stressful and exploitive for service users to hold devolved responsibility for managing the employment of their own personal assistants;

■ there are technical difficulties, for instance: regulating and checking criminal records (the Criminal Records Bureau check is referred to in Chapter Three); being responsible for health and safety issues in the home (mandatory if more than five personal assistants are employed by the service user); and overseeing the training and national insurance contributions of all personal assistants employed by service users and carers.

What do social workers do?

Social work practice takes place in aspects of people's lives that may be difficult, problematic and sometimes controversial. There are continuing debates about what social workers actually do and what they should do. There is a tension between their many different roles, illustrated in Figure 1.3, which is based on a flip chart from a discussion carried out with a group of student social workers.

Figure 1.4 shows the wide continuum covered by social work practice. Three particular points are highlighted, but in reality there are many major social work activities that could be placed on this continuum.

Figure 1.3: Roles of social workers

Service provider

Creative thinker   Risk assessor and auditor

Mediator   Therapist

Team member
                        Enabler and empowerer

Navigator   Activist

Counsellor   Authority figure and intervener

Gatekeeper of resources   Broker

Adviser about services   Information giver

Advocate   Designer of package to meet assessed needs

Designer of social care system

Figure 1.4: Continuum of social work practice

Intervention work	Change work	Advocacy work
(Directing people)	(Facilitating)	(Empowering)

However, the three points – intervention, change and advocacy work – do bring to the fore the very different nature of the range of roles performed by social workers.

Intervention work

Social workers have important responsibilities that necessitate them applying the law, and sometimes these applications are enforced on people. This is particularly the case in safeguarding work with children, families and adults, and using the powers of mental health legislation to prevent people with serious mental illnesses or disorders harming themselves or others.

Change work

Much of social work falls into this middle ground, concerned with facilitating and enabling people so that change occurs in their lives. A common element in most, if not all, of this work is that it is built around the notion of the helping or therapeutic relationship between the practitioner and the client. Many of the roles traditionally lying close to social work (therapies of many kinds, task-centred work, crisis intervention and counselling, referred to below) – lie under this heading of change work, or 'relationship work' as we may prefer to call it.

Task-centred work

Task-centred work was created in the late 1960s (Reid, 1963; Reid and Shyne, 1969). It focuses on the practitioner working with the agreement of the service user and the carer to identify a way forward with problems and to find short-term ways of tackling short-term problems (Reid and Epstein, 1972; Doel and Marsh, 1992).

Crisis intervention

Crisis intervention is rooted in the work of Gerald Caplan (1961, 1964) in the 1960s. Golan (1978) sets out its theory and practice, based on the notion of crises as happenings that disturb the equilibrium of an individual, group or organisation that can lead to stresses if the problems they create are not surmounted. Crisis intervention consists of the different actions and treatments designed to interrupt the crisis and to minimise or prevent harm arising from it (Adams, 2007, p 420).

Counselling

Counselling and psychotherapy are similar in that they both aim to enable people to deal with their problems and to live more satisfying lives. Terry (1997) illustrates how counselling approaches, such as brief counselling and open-ended counselling, may be used constructively with older people and their carers. Brief counselling is not more superficial because it is time-limited, any more than counselling is more superficial than psychotherapy (Dryden and Feltham, 1992, p 2).

Therapy

Social workers may become involved in a range of therapeutic work. Family therapy and cognitive behavioural therapy are the two most widely known. Family therapy is the general term for approaches to therapeutic work to help the family change, which treat the family as a whole. Cognitive behavioural therapy is a therapeutic approach which mobilises people's thoughts and feelings with a view to enabling them to decide to change their behaviour. Brief therapy is another very widely used approach, often as a way of enabling people to bring about immediate changes in their handling of their problems. Life history work can be important in work with children, young people and adults, including older people suffering from physical impairments and dementia. It entails enabling the person to assemble memories, perceptions and experiences and constructing the story of their life, based on what is important to them. It can be a vital component of therapy, such as helping a person's recovery from the trauma of abuse.

Networking

Networking is a general technique of use in work with individuals, groups, including family groups, and communities. It entails identifying connections between the person and different points of reference of significance to them, interpersonally and socially, and developing purposeful ways of developing them, as part of the services they use. Networking is not just a tool for professionals, but can be an empowering way in which service users and carers change their own lives.

Change work is emotion work

Much social work focusing on bringing about change is what we may call **emotion work**. Traditionally, in relationships, women have taken on more emotion work, paid and unpaid, than men. In childcare and work with adults, as well as in care roles, there is at the very least a substantial overlap between social work and emotion work.

Hochschild (1983) first used the term 'emotion work' to refer to the activities of female airline cabin crew when attempting to maintain passengers' moods while on flights. James (1989) notes that girls and women are socialised into being skilful in empathising with other people's emotions. These studies are more associated with paid work. Duncombe and Marsden (1995) have researched relationships between heterosexual partners. They chart the process of relationships in which women take on a disproportionate burden of the emotion work. In the early stages of a relationship, the partners, and especially the women, very much in love, may shelve their doubts. Later in the relationship, their doubts may surface inside them but for the sake of their partner and the world outside the household they still may 'live the myth' of being happily married, whilst beginning to confide their doubts and aspects of unhappiness to friends. The emotional burden of this may entail them in engaging in a 'triple shift' of work, housework and emotion work. The sustained load of this over a period of time may lead to the relationship suffering visibly, or even breaking down altogether.

According to Duncombe and Marsden (1995), to change the fact that, as mentioned above, women take on more of the emotion work in many personal and professional situations, would entail a major reorganisation of childcare and work, as well as a fundamental transformation of heterosexual masculinity.

Simultaneously, there are divisions of gender within some of these occupations, which significantly affect the kinds of roles and responsibilities undertaken by men and by women. These make a difference, for instance, to how a 'social work with children and families team' operates in a children's department. The following **example** shows how this aspect may be worked out in practice.

Example

At management level, the woman who is a team leader may take a less macho approach to leadership and practice. She may encourage practitioners to engage in open and 'feminine' styles of work. This may contrast with the management style of the department. At the practice level, this may entail social workers taking on a range of practice approaches and working styles, from authoritative interventions to counselling and advocacy work with people.

Advocacy work

Social workers are among a range of other people who engage in advocacy. Brandon (1995, p 12) distinguishes between citizen advocacy (a volunteer working with and supporting a devalued person), peer advocacy (one devalued person supporting another) and collective advocacy where people with a shared interest speak up collectively on their own behalf. To this we can add professional advocacy, which is where social workers, lawyers and welfare rights workers, among other professionals, for instance, represent their clients.

Fimister (1986) points out that welfare rights work brings social work into the broader fields of advocacy and social action. This entails influencing policy and practice including lobbying policy makers where appropriate, taking joint action with claimants and combating anti-welfare ideology.

Social work has the potential to empower people. Ideally, in order to make the most of work to empower individual clients, families, groups, organisations and communities, it is preferable for social workers to feel empowered themselves (Adams, 2008b, p 82). In this regard, advocacy and empowerment are closely related. Empowerment is often used as a synonym for facilitating and enabling, but the more authentic forms of empowerment do not involve the social worker relying on having superior power or knowledge over the client and lie closer to working with service users – as co-workers – to enable them to build their own capacity and, where appropriate, engage in social action.

How do we refer to the people with whom social workers work?

We should note three important aspects which apply in social work in particular, but also in other professions working with people. Social workers tend to be sensitive to the terms used to refer to people, not least because much of their professional work is concerned with supporting and safeguarding the interests of people who are vulnerable and whose self-esteem needs to be safeguarded:

■ In work with adults in particular, certain expressions such as 'the mentally ill' and 'the disabled' are not favoured by most professionals. This is because 'the disabled' tends to represent the whole person in terms of a disability, whereas the preferred term 'the disabled person' emphasises the person, one of whose experiences is of being disabled by various 'disabling' features of society. Linked with this, whilst impairment refers to the physical or mental differences between people, the term 'disability' refers to the social oppression and exclusion which exists over and above this.

- Certain words such as 'handicapped', 'crippled', 'defective' and 'dumb' used to be used in general speech as well as legal and procedural documents, but are no longer used in official publications in the UK, being regarded as offensive by professionals and by disabled people themselves.
- Some words such as 'race' are often used in quotation marks to indicate that they have a somewhat problematic status. This is because whereas ethnicity is recognised, the concept of 'race' is a matter for debate among many commentators and professionals, not least because it may imply that a person's identity can be specified in terms of a single, 'pure' racial characteristic, and notions of racial purity and identity are associated with certain racist political and social beliefs.

In the literature about social work, whereas 30 years ago the word 'client' was used for the people on social workers' caseloads, nowadays this word tends only to be used in settings where therapeutic work is the primary purpose of the agency. In most social work agencies, practitioners use the term 'service user' or 'person using services'. It is also common to hear terms such as 'expert through experience' and the term 'carer', or in healthcare settings, 'informal carer'.

Qualities of social workers

It is common to encounter in the social work literature a strong emphasis on the skills practitioners need to acquire. The truth, however, is that to be a social worker also demands certain qualities of the person, a quality being an aspect of the person which is more deep-rooted than a learned skill, so it is more difficult to take on. What qualities do social workers need in order to carry out their broad span of activities? Brandon and Jordan list the qualities of a creative social worker (1979, pp 3-6):

- Self-confidence, that is, not brashness but from security of identity and knowing one's limits.
- Enhanced respect for clients, that is, being not afraid of making a fool of oneself, can enjoy work with people.

- Ability to be flexible, that is, not 'doing what comes naturally' but giving help to others in a disciplined yet creative way.
- Ability to identify sensitively with the impotence and hostility that the client may feel.

Complexity of people's lives

Even though in outline human experience is remarkably uniform (some aspect of the life course is a universal human experience), the problems some people experience lie in the detail of that experience.

Social workers are not like professionals whose core professional credibility rests on technical expertise in manipulating the natural world, such as structural engineers who design bridges to carry a specific load under all the anticipated weather and traffic conditions. The subject matter of social workers' practice consists of the stuff of other people's lives. This human material of existence, individual and social, is something we take for granted. The circumstances of people's lives are rooted in universal experiences – birth, death, family life. People who need social work experience the problems arising from these universals more intensely than other people and, for different reasons, may be vulnerable, in need of safeguarding, mentally ill, disabled or similarly in need.

Range of disciplines on which social work draws

Social work is rooted in several disciplines, including psychology, sociology, social policy, law, philosophy and related subjects such as ethics and psychiatry. Much social work touches on problem-ridden aspects of people's lives and their vulnerabilities. The origins of many of these difficulties are social as well as personal. Consequently, discussion of decision making in social work touches the heart of debates about how far the state should provide universal or selective social security and welfare support for people in need and how far professional social workers should intervene in people's lives. In other words, social work is inextricably associated with sociological and political debates.

Tensions in social workers' roles

The complexity of the subject matter of social work and the range of disciplines on which social workers draw lead to the final point of this chapter – that social workers have to manage an awkward tension, between on the one hand, **intervention**, that is, the exercise of responsibilities, duties and powers in local authorities and other (private, voluntary and independent) agencies providing services where procedures have to be followed, and on the other hand, **creative and empowering** practice, that is, enabling people to find new ways to manage, cope with or change their lives (see Figure 1.5).

We can identify three themes linked with the three categories of roles identified: procedures and laws, relationships and change and capacity and independence.

First, social workers follow procedures and implement the law; second, social workers develop professional relationships with people and bring about change; third, social workers empower people to build capacity and to acquire the resources and expertise to achieve independence.

While social work as creative work seems paradoxical, Brandon and Jordan (1979, pp 1-2) argue that social workers themselves perpetuate some of the constraints of which they complain, so there are ways forward. They need to move beyond plain rule following and act imaginatively. The tension between following procedures and acting creatively also reflects the fact that social work draws on both rational and intuitive approaches to understanding people, what England (1986, pp 22-39) calls the basis of its knowledge and skills, used to understand people.

Figure 1.5: Social work: intervention, creative and empowering work

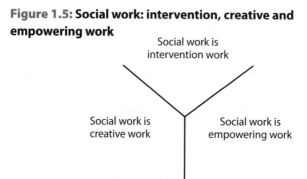

Social work is
intervention work

Social work is
creative work

Social work is
empowering work

'Procedures and laws'

Social work is intervention work	Social workers exercise legal powers on behalf of local authorities and the state. This may entail them acting: – on behalf of a child against an abusive parent – on behalf of a lone mother against her violent partner – to ensure a mentally ill person is compulsorily admitted to a hospital for treatment – to move a vulnerable older person from a hazardous home setting to a residential nursing home
'Relationships and change' **Social work is creative work**	While social work is partly routine, it is also partly creative. In order to carry out their responsibilities and duties, social workers need to engage with the experiences and wishes of people with whom they work and this situates practice in a different place from doing routine, proceduralised tasks. One distinguishing feature of work at a professional level is that it calls on the ability to analyse complex situations and problems, synthesise different types of information and suggest and help to plan new ways forward, to enable a person to manage better, or to change their life. In a real sense, social work is **emotion work**, that is, a creative activity, engaging both the ability of the professional to consider, reason and reflect on problems (rationality), to use one's own experience and feelings as a reflexive means of inspiring new approaches to dealing with them (intuition)
'Capacity and independence' **Social work is empowering work**	Power is an ambiguous idea, in that through its exercise people may either feel oppressed or empowered. The authority of social workers – and their power – derive from four main sources: – their registration with the GSCC – the laws, policies and procedures that they carry out – their personal accountability (to the children, families and adults with whom they work) – their credibility

SUMMARY

This chapter has introduced the nature of social work and provided a basis for examining different aspects of social work practice. It is important to appreciate that while social work draws on many historical and social sources, and some of these are deeply rooted in voluntary and philanthropic movements, the social work profession in today's world is a state-regulated activity which plays a core function in carrying out the legal duties and responsibilities of local authorities regarding the welfare and well-being of children, their families and adults. The industrialisation of the UK and many other western countries from the late 18th century has created social conditions that have disadvantaged some people, and these social inequalities have in many ways been emphasised in the post-industrial late 20th and early 21st century. Social workers contribute to sustaining services which support poorer and more vulnerable children and adults. Social work aims to enable them to cope with their problems and, hopefully, safeguard them from harm.

RECOMMENDED READING

General texts

The following are some basic books that provide an introduction to social work.

The first book in the social work trilogy, dealing with basic, introductory aspects of social work: Adams, R., Dominelli, L. and Payne, M. (eds) (2009) *Social work: Themes, issues and critical debates* (3rd edn), Basingstoke: Palgrave Macmillan.

A useful basic text, covering the main processes, methods and contexts of social work: Coulshed, V. and Orme, J. (2006) *Social work practice: An introduction*, Basingstoke: Palgrave.

A unique book, based on the autobiographical accounts of people who have come into social work from many different backgrounds and directions. It emphasises the view that there is no single, simple definition of social work. It means many different things to different people: Cree, V. (2003) *Becoming a social worker*, London: Routledge.

Arranged alphabetically, this is a valuable reference work of ideas, approaches and practices in social work: Davies, M. (ed) (2000) *The Blackwell encyclopaedia of social work*, Oxford: Blackwell Publishers.

A useful compendium of short articles, introducing the main aspects of social work: Davies, M. (ed) (2002) *The Blackwell companion to social work* (2nd edn), Oxford: Wiley-Blackwell.

A book that introduces many of the ideas and debates that engage existing students and practitioners of social work: Payne, M. (2006) *What is professional social work?* (2nd edn), Bristol: The Policy Press.

A clearly written outline of some of the foundation concepts of social work, such as values, skills and practice: Thompson, N. (2000) *Understanding social work: Preparing for practice*, Basingstoke: Palgrave.

Historical aspects

A fascinating history, showing how psychological ideas have influenced social work: Agnew, E. (2004) *From charity to social work: Mary E. Richmond and the creation of an American profession*, Chicago, Il: University of Illinois.

A good general historical introduction to social work: Payne, M. (2005) *The origins of social work*: *Continuity and change*, Basingstoke: Palgrave.

Values

A sound general introduction to social work values and ethics: Banks, S. (2006) *Ethics and values in social work* (3rd edn), Basingstoke: Palgrave.

The code of ethics of the professional association of social workers: BASW (British Association of Social Workers) (2002) *The code of ethics for social workers*, Birmingham: BASW.

Knowledge base for social work

A text covering relevance to social work of aspects of poverty, social exclusion, families, education and community: Cunningham, J. and Cunningham, S. (2008) *Sociology and social work*, Exeter: Learning Matters.

Social work theories and approaches

A very good introduction to social work approaches and methods: Payne, M. (2005) *Modern social work theory* (3rd edn), Basingstoke: Palgrave.

WEB LINKS

Important report on the state of social care in England
www.cqc.org.uk/_db/_documents/SOSC08%20Report%2008_Web.pdf

Social Care Institute for Excellence: a government-funded source of resources, reviews of practice and research on a range of aspects of social work
www.scie.org.uk/publications/index.asp

Information on poverty and associated debates
www.poverty.org.uk

An authoritative source of data on many relevant personal
and social aspects
www.statistics.gov.uk

2

qualifying programmes in social work

Introduction

Educating and training social workers is a rigorous and challenging process. This chapter and Chapter Three illustrate the pathway into a career as a qualified social worker. This chapter deals with the factual aspects of becoming a social worker, while Chapter Three identifies some key aspects of the process.

Professional education and training in social work

The only route to professional qualification as a social worker in the UK is by undertaking a qualifying programme in higher education that is approved by the registration bodies (GSCC, NISCC, SSSC and CCW for the relevant countries). Most of the courses are at undergraduate level, leading to an honours degree, but a significant number are postgraduate courses, which attract a Master's qualification.

Qualifying as a social worker

The term 'social worker' is a protected title in the UK under the 2000 Care Standards Act, which means that only a suitably qualified and registered social worker can be employed in this role. All staff employed as social workers in the UK must be registered with one of the regulatory bodies (GSCC, NISCC, SSSC or CCW). The Social Work Task Force (2009b) recommended that after completion of the qualifying degree in social work, practitioners should spend a probationary first year, on successful completion of which a licence to practise would be awarded. The UK Social Care Register is the register of people who work in social care (including social work) who have been assessed as suitably qualified to do so. The stages of application are outlined in Table 2.1.

Table 2.1: Stages of application for the qualifying social work programme

Stage	What it entails
Building profile (statement of relevant qualifications and experience)	Spending time building relevant academic qualifications, other qualifications such as driving certificate and suitable work experience, to meet entry requirements
Searching	Identifying preferred degree programmes, chosen on the basis of convenience of location, type of course (for example, whether full-time, work-based or part-time) and other personal factors
Applying	Completing application forms
Selection	Being invited to go through the selection process for a degree programme
Participating	Taking part in the selection procedure
Offer	Being offered a place subject to requirements
Criminal records check	Going through CRB check
Starting course/ induction onto course	Becoming a student (perhaps for the first time)

Acceptance is normally made conditional on a CRB check, which is carried out by the agency to ascertain whether the individual has any history associated with a criminal record.

A wide variety of applicants seek qualification as social workers. Here are four examples giving an indication of the relevant educational and paid and voluntary work experience that is likely to give candidates an advantage when applying.

Example 1

Donna is 27 and has a degree in the social sciences. She has worked as a volunteer in a children's centre.

Example 2

Kal is 25, has worked as a volunteer in several small voluntary agencies, and is currently secretary of the local residents' association.

Example 3

Mel is 40 and worked in residential care with children and adults before fostering several children.

Example 4

Colin is 50, has experienced mental illness, and is now a carer for his partner.

While people's ages have been given in the examples above, a person's age will not normally be taken into account when considering their suitability for employment or education and training. However, other factors will be considered, including

- relevant educational courses in areas such as the social sciences;
- experience of employment in health or social services;
- experience, whether paid or voluntary, of caring for children or adults;
- experience, whether paid or voluntary, of the voluntary sector;
- experience of fostering or adopting children;
- experience, whether paid or voluntary, of community action or community work.

Normally, candidates of any age, including younger applicants who have just completed sixth form or further education, A-levels or their equivalent, will be expected to demonstrate not just that they have relevant educational, life or work experience, but that they can reflect on that experience. I recall an applicant for a social work course being rejected. After he asked for an explanation, he was told that he had not demonstrated the ability to learn from his experience. He responded with the comment: "But I have many years of experience." The answer he received was along the lines that it was not the length of a person's experience that counted but the extent to which they reflected on it and learned from it.

It is increasingly possible to find work as a volunteer which will equip a person to find out what social work entails and, if they wish subsequently, to apply for a qualifying social work programme. The expansion of the private, voluntary and independent sectors makes this an ever-widening area of opportunity. Some longstanding organisations provide openings for volunteering, such as Community Service Volunteers (CSV). Pilot schemes run by CSV in 'Volunteering in child protection' have now been taken up by some local authorities and offer opportunities for volunteers to really make a difference to families (Williams, 2008, pp 20-1).

Volunteers do not have to register as social workers at this stage. However, student social workers must achieve provisional registration soon after they enrol on a qualifying programme or before working with service users.

Outline of qualifying programme in social work

Prospective students apply for a degree through UCAS (Universities and Colleges Admissions Service), but are also recommended to contact preferred universities of their choice informally before applying, to find out more about the nature of the social work programme they run, features of the structure and contents of the programme and any other local factors. The basic requirements of a qualifying programme in the UK are that through it the student social worker will obtain both an undergraduate degree and full registration as a qualified social worker. The typical qualifying undergraduate programme consists of 360 credits that the student takes in stages. A full-time student takes these over three or four years (single honours degrees in Scotland, for instance, are generally four years long, while those in England and Wales are generally three years), and different universities have different full and part-time programmes, including work-based and blended learning (which uses flexible patterns of study), which means that the qualification is obtained over a longer period. Students who have accumulated credits on an equivalent course of study may be granted credit exemptions (accreditation of prior experiential learning [APEL]; the scheme may be referred to as credit accumulation and transfer [CAT]), which means that they do not have to undertake that portion of the programme for which credit is obtained.

Knowledge and understanding

University or college-based study offers the opportunity to gain the underpinning knowledge and understanding to support practice. This is of two types: direct and indirect (see Table 2.2). Direct in this context means the knowledge and understanding used in practice; indirect means the knowledge and understanding used to support the practitioner.

Table 2.2: **Direct and indirect knowledge and understanding**	
Direct	**Indirect**
Human growth and development	How the court system works
Social work approaches and methods	How social work organisations function
Laws affecting children and adults	Social work office administration
Welfare benefits	Approaches to professional supervision
Poverty and social exclusion	
Note: These are examples only and are not meant to be a comprehensive statement.	

Practice education

A significant part of every qualifying programme consists of practice education, that is, learning while in work settings and engaged in supervised practice. Normally, these practice learning opportunities (PLOs) are spaced out so that three take place, one in each stage of the programme. The first is linked with a 'fitness to practise' test, which screens out at an early stage anybody assessed as unfit to practise or whose practice is judged as potentially dangerous.

Agency-based practice and university- or college-based study are combined on these courses, practice learning being divided into different periods, either as complete blocks of time in an agency or several days a week running alongside spending the remainder of the week in the university or college.

Practice in agencies forms an integral part of the qualifying social work programme, and the lengths of placements vary. There is usually a short placement near the start of the programme, perhaps 20 working days in length, and two longer placements in the second and third years (or their equivalents, on a part-time programme, which may take from four to six years).

A practice assessor usually acts as the student's day-to-day, or 'continuous' supervisor of this PLO. There may also be an offsite practice educator. Supervision of the student is intended to ensure that the student can demonstrate a critical understanding of social work values, principles and approaches, and of the registration body's code of practice (COP)(the name of the registration body differs in each country of the UK – see the end of this chapter) and meet the relevant National Occupational Standards (NOS), that is, demonstrate that they can apply them in practice.

The student normally uses a form as a checklist to ensure that the occupational standards are covered and this is known as the NOS assessment form, or some similar title. The student illustrates each element of practice on this form by giving at least one example, and the personal assessor signs that section of the form to certify that this is suitable and sufficient evidence of meeting this standard.

Assessment tasks linked with practice learning

The student carries out several assessment tasks during and at the end of each placement. The way these are organised varies on different courses. The following will probably appear in one form or another.

Placement report

The student is likely to be required to complete a report containing a summary of the agency, its organisation and work, its philosophy and values and how service users participate in it. The report will normally include details of the work the student has done and examples of the records of supervision by the personal assessor.

Reflecting on practice learning

Invariably, there will be a requirement for the student to demonstrate the ability to write in a reflective way about the practice learning experience. It is here that the student learns that reflection is more than simply looking back at what has been done and involves thinking about the meaning and the personal and professional impact of the experience.

It is common for a student to use graphic (illllustration) techniques to help to identify important aspects of what has been learned. For instance, the student may draw a spider chart on a large sheet of paper, using different colours to highlight the relative importance of different themes. A more elaborate figure uses further lines to extend certain sub-categories of learning; for instance, in giving evidence in court, further learning about assertiveness and confidence building can be added, linked also with therapeutic work (see Figure 2.1).

Observed practice

The student will be required to provide other evidence of practice expertise, through observed practice. There will probably be six of these observed practices and the student may be required to ensure that a minimum number (for instance, four) are of an encounter with a service user.

Figure 2.1: What has been learned (spider chart)

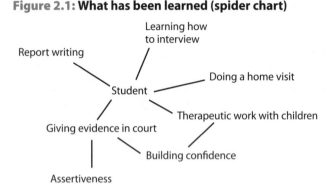

Case study linking theory with practice, critical reflection, reflective study or integrated practice study

There is likely to be a piece of work that expects the student to integrate theory with practice. The student will normally be expected to select one or more pieces of practice and to write about how theoretical perspectives and understandings of social work approaches have informed the practice.

The written work is likely to require the student to discuss how social work values and ethics have been expressed in relation to the professional code of practice, how anti-discriminatory and anti-oppressive perspectives have been demonstrated and how theory and practice relate in the selected approaches used in work with people.

The following are the kinds of criteria likely to be applied when assessing the student's performance:

■ showing evidence of a grasp of relevant policy;

- demonstrating understanding and the appropriate use of the law in practice;
- demonstrating reflective skills;
- showing sensitivity and self-awareness, particularly of how the student's own background affects practice;
- showing the ability to reflect critically on the student's own practice.

Evaluating the practice learning experience

Once the placement has finished, the student normally has the opportunity to complete a written evaluation of the entire experience (see Table 2.3).

Assessment and standards of attainment

The work done by a student is assessed, using general criteria which are applied in an holistic way, but which can be broken down along the lines of Figure 2.2.

Assessment criteria are applied progressively, in two ways:

- In order to achieve a higher mark, the student has to perform at a higher level.
- As the course progresses, the standard expected of the student is raised. The first of these – judgement about performance – is made in terms of achievement against specific criteria relating to the particular assignment, and general criteria (see Table 2.4).

On the whole, the distinctive element of the assessment of student social workers' expertise is that by the time they qualify they should be able to synthesise or integrate these three elements: the knowledge they draw on and how well they understand it; their ability to reflect and analyse what is going on; and their ability to present their views both verbally and in writing (records and reports).

Table 2.3: **Evaluating the placement experience**	
Placement started on time	Yes/No
Placement learning corresponded with agreed opportunities	Yes/No
Student was given all relevant essential information in advance	Yes/No
Student happy with process of allocating the placement	Yes/No
Learning agreement signed by student, tutor, personal assessor and practice supervisor in advance	Yes/No
Planned induction given	Yes/No
Planned induction was satisfactory	Yes/No
Accountability and roles clear	Yes/No
Learning needs met	Yes/No
Supervision provided	Yes/No
Placement assessment satisfactory	Yes/No
Any other comments	
Note: This is a sample checklist of aspects on which the student may be asked to comment.	

Figure 2.2: Components of assessment criteria

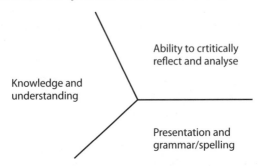

Ability to crtitically reflect and analyse

Knowledge and understanding

Presentation and grammar/spelling

Registration and regulation of social workers

The social care workforce is regulated in each of the four countries by a separate body. Registration of the wider social care workforce in Scotland, Wales and Northern Ireland is already proceeding, although at a slightly different rate in each country, but in England it has not

Table 2.4: General criteria for assessment of student's assignments

	Knowledge and understanding	Reflection and analysis	Presentation and grammar
First class degree (70%)	Wider ranging; no gaps in knowledge; original ideas	Concepts clear; theories; creative	Coherent and clearly explained
Upper second-class degree (60-69%)	Shows very good understanding; key aspects explained	Very good application of concepts and reflection	Clearly structured; concise use of language
Lower second class degree (50-59%)	Evidence of good understanding; a few gaps in knowledge	Good use of reflection and concepts	Structured, with appropriate use of language most of the time
Third class degree (40-49%)	Minimal grasp of knowledge; basic understanding	Barely adequate reflection and analysis	Basic structure with some weaknesses
Fail (below 40%)	Little evidence of relevant reading or understanding	Lack of evidence of reflection or analysis	Poorly structured and incoherent

as yet begun. Social workers practise according to a code of practice published by the GSCC, which maintains a register of qualified and appropriately experienced social workers. After acceptance on to a qualifying programme in social work, students apply for provisional registration with the GSCC. This includes a CRB check, and until both are completed satisfactorily a student cannot proceed on to any practice placements working with people in social work agencies.

Values, principles and codes of ethics

Biestek's (1961) writing about the principles of casework has stood the test of time remarkably well. We can distil the most important of his principles into five considerations, to which many practising social workers would adhere today:

■ individualisation: treating the person as a unique individual;
■ acceptance: accepting the person as he or she is;
■ non-judgementalism: not making judgements about whether the person is right or wrong;
■ self-determination: giving the person space in which to help himself or herself;
■ confidentiality: keeping confidential matters which do not breach professional ethics by not being shared.

The **British Association of Social Workers** (BASW) acts in some ways like a trades union although in fact it lies closer to a professional body. There is no trades union as such for social workers, although some practitioners regard other unions as suitable to join. BASW publishes a **code of ethics** (BASW, 2002, p 2) that sets out five **basic values** as follows:

■ human dignity and worth
■ social justice
■ service to humanity
■ integrity
■ competence.

These generate principles (BASW, 2002, pp 2-7), summarised in Table 2.5.

The GSCC publishes two codes of practice, one for practitioners and the other for managers (GSCC, 2002a, 2002b).

National Occupational Standards

National Occupational Standards for social work (Topss UK Partnership, 2004) is the published statement specifying the performance expected of social workers in their different roles. It is published by Topss (Training Organisation for the Personal Social Services), which was replaced in 2002 by Skills for Care, one of the Sector Skills Councils (SSCs):

- SSSC: www.sssc.uk.com
- CCW: www.ccwales.org.uk
- NISCC: www.niscc.info
- Skills for Care, the government's agency in England (SfC): www.skillsforcare.org.uk

By the end of the qualifying programme, the staff will have assessed:

- the student's knowledge and understanding of the code of practice;
- the extent to which the student has achieved the relevant NOS key roles;
- the student's observed practice.

Table 2.5: Values and principles of social work

Values	Principles
Human dignity and worth	Respecting people's human rights Ensuring dignity Promoting well-being and autonomy Protecting service users
Social justice	Distributing resources to meet human needs Ensuring fair access to services Promoting social development Tackling structural disadvantage
Service to humanity	Putting service to humanity before personal aims Informing people so they can make complaints Enabling people to participate to meet their aims Enabling service users to participate in practice
Integrity	Ensuring private conduct does not compromise fulfilment of professional responsibilities Being honest and accurate Setting and enforcing professional boundaries Avoiding personal or intimate relationships with service users or colleagues
Competence	Identifying, using and sharing knowledge, theory and skill for social work practice Developing competence and expertise Using supervision in continuous professional development Reflecting on how to tackle social problems Engaging in evaluation and research

The NOS key roles comprise values and practice and are published by SfC (Topss, 2004) and can be accessed online (www.skillsforcare.org.uk and www.gscc.org.uk). Table 2.6 shows the main areas of values, ethics and six key roles in the National Occupational Standards (see Table 2.6).

Table 2.6: National Occupational Standards for social work: a summary	
1	Values and ethics
2	Communication skills and information sharing
3	Good social work practice
4	Advocacy
5	Working with other professionals
6	Knowledge
7	Values
Six areas of practice	
1	Prepare for, and work with individuals, families, carers, groups and communities to assess their needs and circumstances
2	Plan, carry out, review and evaluate social work practice, with individuals, families, carers, groups, communities and other professionals
3	Assess and manage risk to individuals, families, carers, groups, communities, self and colleagues
4	Demonstrate professional competence in social work practice
5	Manage and be accountable, with supervision and support, for their own social work practice within their organisation
6	Support individuals to represent and manage their needs, views and circumstances

Values and ethics

1. Communication skills and information sharing – with honesty and clarity.
2. Good social work practice – working professionally, consistently and accountably.
3. Advocacy – empowering people to challenge injustice.
4. Working with other professionals – handle and share information responsibly.
5. Knowledge – use up to date relevant knowledge to protect people's rights.
6. Values – respect and empower people; be honest; respect confidentiality and inform people appropriately; challenge discrimination and put people first.

SUMMARY

This chapter has surveyed the structure of the qualifying programme for social work and has highlighted some of the particular professional requirements that sit alongside, and are integrated with, the requirements associated with a more traditional academic programme in higher education.

RECOMMENDED READING

A book that is widely used by social work students, for the values component of their practice: Thompson, N. (2001) *Antidiscriminatory practice*, Basingstoke: Palgrave.

An excellent critical introduction to social work: Dominelli, L. (2004) *Social work: Theory and practice for a changing profession*, Cambridge: Polity Press.

An introductory book, setting social work in context and exploring in more detail social work with children, disabled people and people with mental health problems: Horner, N. (2009) *What is social work: Contexts and perspectives* (3rd edn), Exeter: Learning Matters.

The codes of practice (published by the GSCC, but identically applicable in each of the four countries of the UK): www.gscc.org.uk/codes/

GSCC (General Social Care Council) (2002) *Code of practice for social care workers*, London: GSCC.

GSCC (2002) *Code of practice for employers of social care workers*, London: GSCC.

The National Occupational Standards incorporate the above-mentioned Codes of Practice. They were published originally by Topss, the training organisation for the personal social services, later replaced by Skills for Care. They are available through the GSCC on the internet: www.gscc.org.uk and then use the quick links down the right hand side of the page.

WEB LINKS

Source of the current direction of policy and practice in social work for Scotland: the 21st Century Social Work Review. A Scottish government view of the potential for the role of social work in society
www.2lc.socialwork.org.uk

3

becoming a social worker

Introduction

Becoming a social worker does not happen at the point where the application form is completed, when the selection process is completed or even when the successful candidate becomes a student on the first day of the course. 'Becoming' is a process that may not even be complete on the day of graduation, because there is a probationary period of practice after qualification. There is a sense in which even after several years of practice, a social worker is still 'becoming'. 'Becoming' could be said to be a career-long process of professional and personal development.

Setting these complications aside, an important early stage in becoming a social worker is to make a successful application for a place on a qualifying degree programme in social work. However, social work courses are over-subscribed by applicants, with some universities receiving four applicants for every place and some even 10. Who are the successful applicants? This chapter looks at how to provide evidence of important qualities and experiences which may be sought by selection panels. Possession of these is likely (although it is not guaranteed) to distinguish the successful from the unsuccessful applicant.

Social work is a reflective profession that requires the practitioner to build on personal qualities of sensitivity and self-awareness, in order to work effectively with other people. This chapter is about how we delve into ourselves in the process of becoming a professional social worker. It helps to prepare for responding to the question from an interviewing panel, or on an application form: 'Why do I want to become a social worker?'

Social work is an art as well as a science

In some ways social work is an art and in others it is a science. That is to say, while social work is rooted in the social sciences and the rationally derived research knowledge that forms the evidence base for practice, it also has roots in the arts and the intuitive understanding drawn on by the creative professions. Another way of putting this is to say that social work practice depends not just on what techniques you know and how you apply them, but on how you bring personal qualities to the job and the kind of person you are. Rather than simply studying the writing that people produce, it is important to seek to understand all the factors, including the social factors, producing this writing. This highlights the importance of not accepting our statements of intent at face value, but questioning our motives, along with other relevant factors. While we may seek instant knowledge and want to acquire some skills quickly, professional expertise does not happen overnight.

How do you convince the interviewer that you have what it takes to justify a place on a social work qualifying programme? You will need to provide evidence of the following six elements:

1. Knowledge and understanding: qualifications may be relevant, and evidence of these emerges in the completed application form. Academic ability is relevant and proof of literacy and numeracy is required. This may involve tests as part of the selection process.
2. Motivation: evidence of your commitment to social work may emerge from your personal statement.
3. Personal qualities: these include ability to empathise with people and initiative, and are likely to emerge from your personal statement.
4. Relevant work experience: this is gathered from the application form and during the selection process. It is likely to include voluntary as well as paid work.
5. Potential to become a student: the willingness to study is difficult to demonstrate if you have been away from formal study for a while. Relevant reading (such as browsing through one or more titles listed at the end of Chapter One) will help to demonstrate motivation to learn.

6. Potential to become a practitioner: this is gathered from the personal statement and during the selection process. A key aspect, for instance, is the ability to hold down a job, working under pressure.

The last two of these, in a sense, are more general and include all the others. In order to demonstrate that you have the potential to study and to practise, you need to show that you have some personal qualities, as well as sufficient academic ability, qualifications and relevant experience. What particular personal qualities are the selection panel and those who interview you seeking? They are contained in the phrase 'ability to empathise' and in words such as 'self-awareness', 'sensitivity' and 'reflectiveness'. These are not the only qualities, but they are crucial ones. They are key ingredients in what is often referred to as 'critically reflective practice' in social work, to which we return in the last major section of this chapter.

Particular professionalism of social work in everyday life

Social work is work with people. Because social workers deal with people's relationships with other people, they encounter on a daily basis the everyday subject matter of people's lives. Inevitably, this means that social work with other people, both colleagues and clients (in many parts of social work clients are referred to as service users or people who use services, and carers are referred to as informal carers), is like holding up a mirror to aspects of our own experience. Social workers encounter other people who are vulnerable and in need and because the problems besetting them are linked with universal life experiences, they are touched by these experiences themselves. It is vital that social workers can make connections at these times and separate their own responses to these from their practice with other people. This is part of the professionalism of social work and it is one of the aspects that distinguishes professional from personal relationships. We relate to other people as acquaintances, friends and relatives, but we are employed to develop professional relationships with service users, and while the subject matter of people's lives is common to all situations, in our professional work we learn to manage our personal responses and, while learning from them, segregate them from our professional practice.

Reflexivity

An important contribution to our ability to practise social work, and probably the most important contribution, is made by us when we explore our own histories, identities and motivation to practise. This is important for several reasons, the most crucial of which is our ability to ensure that we can do the job with help from our own knowledge, experience and emotions, rather than these hindering us. It helps to ensure this, if we can understand ourselves. **Reflexivity**, therefore, is the term used to refer to the ability to know ourselves while on the journey to understanding others.

Students are often asked to undertake a reflective diary during their professional education and training course in social work. This can be revealing, in that it may be the first time the student has set down in writing some reflections that have great personal significance. In part, this may be because experiences during the course have brought aspects of their life back to the surface of present-day reflection, in the light of what they have now experienced, read and discussed. During the period in the mid-1980s, when child and adult abuse were being discussed widely for the first time in some parts of the UK, we realised as tutors the necessity to offer one-to-one counselling opportunities to any students after the lectures and seminars on these topics.

Transformative learning: drawing out personal biographies

I realised the importance of coming to terms with personal experience very early in my work with other people. In 1978, Mezirow gathered a cluster of women's accounts of their personal histories and adult learning and used these as the starting point for his ideas about transformative learning that are still influential today. One powerful means by which we used this approach at college in Hull, on an in-service one day a week course with social care workers and wardens of sheltered housing, was for my colleague Dilys Page to encourage the students to spend time preparing the story of their history and how they came into social care work. Sharing these experiences, sometimes with poster presentations to each other, led to some powerful expressions of issues and barriers, encountered and not always overcome – of class, gender, age, ethnicity and disability. It can be invaluable to repeat this process more than once during the course. **Narratives** – our personal accounts – help us to make connections between our experiences and our later reflections, as well as to make connections with the wider social setting.

Ledwith and Springett (2010) begin their book on participatory practice with a brief account of their own histories which connect with their practice, and throughout the book use different stories as a core means of demonstrating the importance of people's life experiences as critical influences on their practice and the way they understand – or, as we say in the social sciences, theorise – it.

Creating a personal statement

It is helpful to become used to reflecting, and perhaps one of the earliest and most crucial pieces of work the intending social worker does is to write their personal statement supporting their application for a place on a qualifying programme.

As a way of helping the reader to grasp what is entailed in this, I set out below some key aspects of my own biography, not just to inform how I came into social work, but also to illustrate how you, the reader, could go about constructing your own personal statement at this early stage in your journey into social work. It is important, however, to say two things about this biographical note at the start.

Writing in the first person

It is important to feel confident enough about the relevance of our personal experiences and reflections to include ourselves in what we write. A well-known academic who advocates this approach, Bob Pease, Professor of Social Work at Deakin University, Melbourne, Australia, tells me when we discuss this that he always writes in the first person, as a matter of principle. It is necessary to acknowledge that everything we think, all our judgements, and our practice, relate to ourselves. It is a denial of an aspect of social reality to distance ourselves by using the third person – 'he or she' – or by using the passive mood – 'It is felt that…' or 'It was decided…'.

Biography: authenticity rather than mere factual accuracy

The biography is not a fact, but a narrative based on perceptions and experience. A narrative is an account, a story. I do not like the word 'story' in that it was often used when I was a child as a way of dismissing what was said as untrue: 'Don't tell stories!'

What I mean by biography relates to a well-established body of historical research known as oral history and to the traditional activity of story-telling that is more common in pre-industrial societies. Oral historians collect people's accounts, usually by recording them and transcribing their words afterwards. The point often made by oral historians is that it is vital to gather people's first accounts, since in repeated retelling they often change the story, leaving out some details and embellishing others. However, what is more important from the viewpoint of the narrative in biographical work with people is not whether particular details are factually correct, but its **authenticity**, by which I mean the significance to the storyteller, the meaning given to personal experience.

In other words, in writing biographically, the authenticity of the biography transcends questions of its factual accuracy. This is not to say that I set out deliberately to mislead, but simply that what I emphasise about, say, a meeting with somebody, is important to me, but it may not be important to them in the same way.

My biographical note: How I came into social work

In answer to the question 'What made you apply to become a social worker?' I have written the account below, as an example. The references I have chosen are to the people and books that have influenced me. So you will find that some of these are quite idiosyncratic and personal.

This is inevitable, given the task I set myself. Hopefully, when you have read this, you will feel able to carry out your own biographical account of your own journey into social work, and, over the years to come, you will feel confident enough to keep returning to it and rewriting it, as you re-interpret your judgements in the light of further reflection and experience. It is an open and unending process, with no final, 'correct' answer.

Example

As a young person I had some mental health problems, which I attempted to deal with without talking to anybody. When I reached university, I visited the student counselling service, but did not receive the referral or the help I wanted, so I continued to attempt to cope with them alone. It was many years later that I understood the force of a remark made by the American writer about illness, Susan Sontag, in her essay 'Notes on "Camp"': 'Many things in the world have not been named; and many things, even if they have been named, have never been described' (Sontag, 1966, p 275). To have the knowledge many decades later that the disabling symptoms from my mid-teens onwards, of staring into the mirror and counting every hair on my head, as well as those that were falling out, had a name – body dysmorphic disorder – was reassuring but somewhat late in the day. The disorder had, in effect, robbed me of several hours each day. By the time I found out, my own baldness was causing less anxiety as men around me had also gone bald with the passing years, and the eating disorders that I had lived with for so long had diminished.

I chose to study a general degree in a handful of disparate subjects that interested me: English literature, economics, music and Latin. I was drawn, not surprisingly, towards society's attempts to contain deviance in general and mental health problems in particular. My social history studies highlighted poverty and drew me towards the prison and mental hospital systems.

I turned down an immediate referral to a place on the university's social work training course. I visited a youth centre run by Gwilym Morgan, vicar of St Phillips, Salford. He believed that the centre should be allowed to run its course with a particular generation, perhaps close down and then be re-opened by another generation of young people. He enthused over Sheelagh Delaney's new play, 'A taste of honey', and was spending money he saved from giving up smoking on small sketches by a little known local artist called Lowry, who had a gift for characterising the lives of working-class people. These were revelatory views of a world into which I moved on graduation, and in which I now worked as assistant 'cellarman' in a non-residential hotel in south Manchester, where I had already met at least one employee with serious mental health problems. From my reading, I recognised in him immediately some symptoms of schizophrenia.

I spent hours when not at work walking round Strangeways Prison, reading about penal institutions. I wrote to request an interview at the regional office of the Prison Department and was advised in a light-hearted way to take a holiday in Spain and return to the Open Competition for the Civil Service to enter immediately at governor grade level. I ignored this advice and applied to become a prison officer. I was interviewed at Winchester, the closest prison to my home town, and was offered a place there. I turned this down and requested a large London prison. Within months, I had moved as a newly appointed prison officer, to Pentonville Prison.

At Pentonville, I became aware that most of D Wing was occupied by hundreds of homeless men, many of whom had problems of addiction to drink and mental health problems. I saw prison as totally inappropriate and spent much time after work engaged with what to do about it. I went to Camberwell, the DHSS Reception Centre, and although I did not stay overnight, while queuing up for the evening meal I met Tony Parker, author of many books written in people's own words, in the queue, and we discussed how to understand the experience of people who offended and were homeless. I visited Norman Ingram Smith, the inspirational vicar at St Martin's in the Fields in Trafalgar Square, who sat with me in the crypt which he had opened up as a refuge for homeless people. He explained to me how he felt closest to a man recovering from an alcoholic binge when they had both sat together being sick into the same bucket. I visited Michael Sorensen and discussed with him the prison visitors scheme which he ran from Blackfriars Settlement in South London. In the evening, I visited Reverend Chad Varah's newly set up Samaritans centre at his church. I visited the new property of the Simon Community, newly created by the former probation officer Anton Wallach Clifford, who I later met walking across Hampstead Heath, and discussed the practice of trusting recently arrived residents with the keys of the building and, shortly after, with giving out money from the locked cabinet. Breaking down the distinction between staff and residents was felt to be helpful. This was something I later found inspirational in visiting Botton Village, the community in rural North Yorkshire run on the utopian principles of Rudolf Steiner. In North London I met the barrister Mervyn Turner, who visited prisoners at Pentonville, and went to his home for open house on a Saturday night, where any ex-prisoners with whom he had worked had an open invitation. As a group who had never been together in this situation before, we discussed alternatives to prison intensively and at length. I was acutely aware of the century or more of incarceration these men shared between them. Mervyn had founded the chain of Norman Houses for prisoners' aftercare in London and was talking of the need for a community, perhaps in Wales, as a radical alternative to prison for people with problems of alcohol abuse.

I was preoccupied with the number of prisoners at Pentonville who were clearly suffering very serious mental health problems, for which there was no provision. The psychiatrists who visited were merely assessing, not engaged in treatment. I was invited to join a regular meeting of psychiatrists from mental hospitals such as Claybury Hospital, Woodford Green in Essex and the

Henderson Hospital which was running as a therapeutic community, and we discussed therapeutic regimes and their difficulties. I volunteered to help John Bazalgette at regular meetings with young men who had been in trouble, in his explorations of their relationships with authority that led to a well-known book, *Freedom, authority and the young adult* (Bazalgette, 1971).

As a prison officer, I had fantasised that my feeling of total powerlessness in this huge institution would disappear if and when I became a governor. When, seven years later, I became acting governor of a young offenders' institution, I still felt pretty powerless, aware that when I made decisions, the prison officers could undermine and ignore them as soon as my back was turned. This paradox, plus reading and discussing custodial punishments with many penal reformers, convinced me that the best option for the majority of prisons (about three quarters) housing very minor young and adult offenders, many of whom had mental health problems, would be to close them down and use the money to provide treatment and real support in the community.

In the meantime, as acting governor, I was sat in the governor's office in the young offender's institution reading Erving Goffman (1968a) on the characteristics of total institutions and David Matza (1969) on the processes of becoming labelled as a deviant and the further ('secondary') deviance that results from this stigma. At the time of forced feeding of IRA hunger-striking prisoners in the early 1970s, I made the decision that I could not continue in the role of governor, because I would refuse to give this particular order.

The Home Office agreed to support me in taking a postgraduate diploma in social studies. I undertook a work placement as a social work assistant at the newly reorganised York Social Services Department, where I worked with social workers dealing with older and disabled people, followed by a similar placement with the West Yorkshire Probation Service where I met Martin Rowntree, probation officer, quaker, innovator. He had recently founded a centre in Pontefract that was later used by the Home Office as a model for new day training centres. Next door was a club he had founded with the aim of keeping young people who offended out of penal custody and helping them make the transition to law-abiding adulthood. We visited the club together one evening and I found out that it had no leader. A few weeks later, I resigned from my post as prison governor to run that club, attracting grants for youth leaders from the Youth Service, for instructors from the Adult Education Service and for social workers and activity leaders from social services, the premises and core staff being maintained by Barnardo's. It was a natural step soon afterwards for me to take a postgraduate qualification as a social worker.

During this period, I experienced two particularly creative sequences of social work practice – one working with Bebe Speed, an extraordinarily creative social worker with particular interest in family therapy, as part of a multidisciplinary team on the psychiatric ward of Leeds General Infirmary; the other working in the student unit with the inspirational David Sawdon, at the CVS, York. There I undertook a survey of the experience of youth unemployment and, through David's contacts with Colin and Mog Ball who led the government's policy initiatives on rising youth unemployment, this was published as an article (Adams and Sawdon, 1979) in the national journal *Actions*, before the year was out.

By that time, I had started to write books about social work with young offenders and self-help and empowerment (Adams, Allard, Baldwin and Thomas, 1981; Lindenfield and Adams, 1984, 1990), and to explore radical ideas in adult education. I met Ralph Ruddock, then in the Adult Education Department, University of Manchester, and spent several years debating with him while he introduced me to the internationally acclaimed writing of Ettore Gelpi and Paulo Freire, and this was the beginning of

> my explorations of transformative practice. This was the point
> when I became committed to writing the history of prison riots
> in Britain and the US (Adams, 1992) and doing research on
> protests by children and young people, particularly those in
> various institutions concerned with schooling (Adams, 1991). It
> would be true to say that it is the work of Freire to which I return
> constantly, more so than any other non-fiction books I have read.

Readers could check this personal statement against the six elements
identified earlier in this chapter, to see how far it matches up to them.

So far we have considered how we reflect on our experiences prior
to the qualifying programme. Now we consider what is involved in the
process of becoming qualified, while on the programme.

Learning how to become a critically reflective practitioner

The goal outlined in the lists of values and practice standards in Chapter
Two can best be achieved by developing a particular style of practice,
and this requires the practitioner to be critical and reflective. Much of
the qualifying programme focuses on how the student can achieve this.
In the first place, there are several components of the learning process.

Learning social work

Students undergoing professional qualification programmes need to gain
critical understanding on their journey to acquiring practice expertise.
The learning process on the qualifying course is more complex than
that, since it requires the student to integrate several different aspects
in order to develop expertise (Figure 3.1).

Expertise is the product of the student's experience and learning.
Expertise is the term used to refer to the ability to demonstrate working
purposefully and productively with people. **Previous experience** – both
personal experience and experience gained through work – is a much

Figure 3.1: Components of expertise

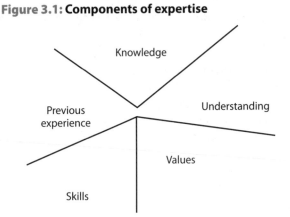

valued commodity on social work qualifying programmes, provided the applicant shows evidence on being able to reflect on, and learn from, this experience. At interview, as well as in completing the written application, the prospective social worker will take the opportunity to show how relevant this experience is to the current application. **Learning** – the term used to refer to acquired knowledge, understanding and skills – is a combination of knowledge, understanding, skills and commitment to professional values. Approximately half of the undergraduate social work programme, which leads to a degree and the professional qualification in social work, is spent in **supervised practice** in an agency, supervised by an appropriately qualified and experienced practice educator. Lishman (2007) provides a useful guide to the practice educator's threefold responsibilities, which consist of

- acting as a supportive guide to the student social worker;
- enabling the student to learn while in practice;
- contributing to the assessment of the student, in all the areas of practice necessary to meet the occupational standards for social work.

Developing as a critically reflective practitioner

During the qualifying programme the student social worker will be faced with the task of learning how to become a critically reflective practitioner. There are four main components to what the student draws on when reflecting:

■ particular experiences of practice;
■ reading about social work (not just newspaper articles, but reports of research, for instance, in social work journals);
■ discussion with colleagues;
■ receiving professional supervision.

Most are self-explanatory, but the last component needs further examination.

What is supervision?

Social workers need professional supervision, not just during their qualifying education and training but when they qualify and enter practice. **Supervision** is the term used to refer to the process of structured critical reflection on practice, conducted through the medium of a professionally qualified independent person acting as reflector, both in monitoring the content and relevance and in evaluating the quality of critical reflection. Supervision has the potential to be used to help five major aspects of the student's progress to be explored in a structured way and monitored:

1. Professional
2. Personal
3. Educational
4. Managerial
5. Administrative

The first three could be regarded as more in the student's interest and the last two as more in the interests of the supervisor or line manager, bearing in mind that sometimes the supervisor will be the line manager and sometimes a person not in the line of management, which latter option many professionals prefer.

Pen picture

Mathias has a bias towards working with the male children in the family, rather than the female children. His supervisor picks this up during regular supervision sessions and discusses this with him. He is able to identify factors contributing to this bias and to counteract them. At first he was defensive about this, but he later acknowledged this and is now grateful for the opportunity to reach a better understanding, learn from experience and improve his practice.

The activity of supervision, ideally, is safe for the student practitioner, being the place where, as O'Sullivan notes (1999, p 37), ideas can be tested out by the student and different perspectives (theoretical views of, or approaches) to a problem or situation tested out. Supervision is capable of being used flexibly, as the following list of potential applications illustrates:

- to bridge theory and practice;
- to enable the student to model (test out in practice) listening and being listened to;
- to explore how the quality of reflection in practice is maintained;
- to enhance personal learning;
- to develop understanding;
- to facilitate team development;
- to encourage personal and professional development;
- to release tensions and identify factors contributing to stress;
- to enable the line manager to maintain oversight (or even take control!);
- to enable the student to maintain a questioning approach;
- to enable the student to monitor reflection and use of ideas in practice;
- to improve the health and safety aspects of practice (that is, develop safer practice).

The process of supervision heightens the practitioner's awareness of issues and confidence in developing greater expertise. This is also achieved through a combination of practice, reading research reports and commentaries on practice, talking with colleagues, attending short courses, seminars, talks and lectures. The journey towards critically reflective practice is continuous, and most commonly reflectiveness is written about as a state of being rather than something the practitioner does which enables a 'quick fix', like finding a puncture in a tyre and mending it. Becoming reflective and critical is likely to remain a permanent state of becoming. This is quite a frustrating idea from the viewpoint of the person who likes there to be a straightforward solution to a family's or an individual's problem, but as we know from everyday life experience, most life problems are not able to be solved in this way. Hence, the model of reflective practice as constant and unending lies closer to reality than seems the case at first.

These integrative ingredients of critically reflective practice are represented diagrammatically in Figure 3.2. **Integration** is the term used to describe an act or a process of combining parts so that they fit together and form a whole. Integration sounds like a finished whole, while the word 'integrative' is more realistic because it refers to an ongoing process.

Figure 3.2: Ingredients of integrative activity

Becoming research-minded

We have mentioned research. It is important for the practitioner to be confident in reading about the research being carried out into different aspects of practice. This does not mean that the social worker has to carry out research into practice. It is important to be able to read, to understand and discuss research findings, for instance, research that poses the question as to whether particular practice is effective or not. The research may ask in what ways the practice works particularly well and what can be learned from this and applied in future practice. Good evaluative research of this kind actually also asks how strong the research has been – a very self-critical question and one that is difficult to tackle.

SUMMARY

This chapter has tackled two central aspects of becoming a qualified social worker. The first is the task of preparing a personal statement. The second is becoming a critical and reflective practitioner.

RECOMMENDED READING

An introduction to the ideas concerning developing as a critical practitioner: Adams, R., Dominelli, L. and Payne, M. (eds) (2009) Critical practice in social work (2nd edn), Basingstoke: Palgrave (see, in particular, chapter 1).

A detailed exploration of ideas and practices involved in critical reflection: Fook, J. and Gardner, F. (2007) Practising critical reflection: A resource handbook, Maidenhead: Open University Press.

WEB LINKS

The UK professional bodies for social care all set out detailed information on how to become a social worker.

Care Council for Wales
www.ccwales.org.uk/qualifications-and-careers/social-work-degree/training

General Social Care Council (England)
www.gscc.org.uk/Become+a+social+worker/

Northern Ireland Social Care Council
www.niscc.info/a_career_in_social_work-38.aspx

Scottish Social Services Council
www.sssc.uk.com/sssc/social-service-careers/training-as-a-social-worker.html

organisation, legal basis
and regulation of social work

Introduction

This chapter examines the basis for organising and providing social work services and for social workers to use their legal powers. It also indicates how social workers practise beyond the scope of legal duties, in carrying out the responsibilities of the state for supporting and empowering people and, in some circumstances, preventing them from becoming subject to the legal duties of local authorities and the state.

How social work is organised

In the UK social work is organised and administered through local authorities, which provide some services directly and commission others from a hugely important and ever-growing range of private, voluntary and independent organisations and agencies.(I thought important to refer to PVI because used quite widely)

There are different organisational arrangements for social services in the four countries of the UK as powers are devolved differently in each, although some laws passed in Westminster by the English Parliament apply throughout the UK.

Scotland has its own parliament, can pass its own primary legislation and is fully responsible for social care and social work. In Wales, much legislation passed by Parliament in London also applies, but the Department for Health and Social Services (DHSS) in Wales is responsible to the Welsh Assembly Government, for policy and practice in health and social services. In Northern Ireland, the former four health and social services boards have merged into the Department of Health, Social Services and Public Safety (DHSSPS), which is responsible for commissioning health and social services, and five health and social care trusts which provide the services.

This book does not go into all the detailed differences in the four countries at every stage, but some distinctive differences need noting. In England, the separation of adults' and children's services is apparent in most local authorities, although some have re-merged them. In Scotland, social work services are the responsibility of social work departments and in some local authorities services for adults and children are together while in others they are separate. (A local authority is an administrative unit of local government.)

Changes in UK social work

In the 21st century, there have been government-led initiatives to improve the image of social workers and to improve their contribution to social services for children and their families and for adults. In Scotland, a major review of social work – the 21st-century review – was commissioned in 2004 (Scottish Executive, 2004), its major recommendations were published in 2006 (Scottish Executive, 2006) and within the following year were adopted. In summary, the report proposed that the expertise of social workers is highly valued and relevant to the needs of our changing society, but the best is not being made of it. A series of measures were set out to build the capacity of the social work workforce and support this through central government and local authorities. In England, the report by Lord Laming in March 2009 (Laming, 2009) following the scandal reported in the mass media over the death of Baby Peter led to the Westminster government publishing its response and strategy (HM Government, 2009). A report sponsored jointly by four major government agencies on the roles and tasks of social workers was only published in March 2008 (GSCC et al, 2008), but was never endorsed at ministerial level. It concluded that social work makes a crucial contribution to tackling people's complex issues through relationships with them, work with other professionals and work in the wider community. Following the public backlash of the Baby Peter scandal, the English government set up a Social Work Task Force whose interim findings in May 2009 (Social Work Task Force, 2009a) reported that social workers felt undervalued and not adequately recognised or understood by the general public. Their final report recommended measures to raise the profile of social work as a profession by making education, training and further professional development more robust (Social Work Task Force, 2009b). These have been driven by two sets of factors:

1. *Policy changes as part of the modernisation of public services:* the incoming Labour government of 1997 introduced policies to modernise health and social services and these have affected services for disabled, mentally ill and older people. In England, following the direction of policy in Northern Ireland, adult social services for disabled people, older people (including safeguarding and dementia services) and mentally ill people were becoming more integrated with health services.

2. *Changes in response to successive scandals and identified shortcomings of children's services:* a succession of inquiries into failures of child protection services over a 30-year period culminated in legislation in the early 21st century that significantly reformed the structure and organisation of services for children and families. By 2008, under the 2004 Children Act, new local authority children's services departments were created in England, combining former education and social services departments; similar changes took place in social services for children in Wales, although generic social services departments remained responsible for services for children, families and adults. In Scotland, social work with young offenders remains based in social work departments. In other countries of the UK, since the last quarter of the 20th century there has been a growing divide between social work and the criminal justice system.

Partnership working

The title of a government publication (DH, 1999d, HM Government, 2006) on one form of partnership, between agencies and professionals – *Working together* – captures in these two words a crucial feature of effective partnership. Social workers often act as coordinators of interprofessional practice, since the knowledge base of social work draws on many disciplines and enables practitioners to cross boundaries between different organisations and professions in their day-to-day work.

Partnerships with the voluntary, private and independent sectors

A growing quantity of work is carried out in partnership with voluntary, private and independent agencies. It is true to say that the shape of this sector is changing as this work develops. New forms of joint working are evolving to keep pace with changing policy and practice. Some private, voluntary and independent providers are social enterprises – businesses that have social objectives into which any surpluses are invested, rather than being taken as profits by entrepreneurs or shareholders. The great bulk of social care is provided through these sectors. Social workers are well placed to act as brokers, advocates and negotiators. They are the 'go-betweens' for both the local authority commissioners of services and the voluntary, private and independent organisations that either work with them now or may potentially work with them in future.

Social workers are at the forefront of expertise in working in partnerships with service users and carers. Much work with vulnerable people in particular requires great expertise, in order to preserve that independence which is so much valued by people, and at the same time ensuring that they have access to resources and services to which they are entitled.

Multidisciplinary work is not a liability. It is a potential strength. This is because bringing in different professions, while it does highlight communication as an issue:

■ reveals communication issues which in any case need tackling;
■ offers the potential benefits of bringing different professional experiences, range of evidence and viewpoints to bear on the case.

The potential range of different partnerships with people who use services and carers is vast. They may take place with individuals, families, groups and communities and it is necessary to consider these in turn, since different issues arise in each case.

The scope and variety of partnerships that operate in the health and social services make it difficult to capture the wealth of arrangements in a short statement. We can use the writing of Douglas to outline four main features shared by many partnerships. We can then build our understanding of partnership in practice by drawing on ideas about team working.

Over and above this, Douglas (2007, p 3) identifies four particular features of such partnerships, which we can apply in social work:

- effective communication between partners;
- structures and systems which enable the partnership to work;
- close collaboration between the partners;
- a focus on a particular activity, for instance, reducing harm to people or promoting people's health and well-being.

Importance of the third sector

Organisations and groups in the third sector make a significant and growing contribution to providing social work services, especially in specialist areas such as childcare and work in particular categories of adult services, such as residential care and palliative care. The term 'third sector' is often used interchangeably with the 'voluntary sector', but, recognising that the voluntary sector is also difficult to define, the scope of the third sector is far wider than this. Terms such as 'voluntary organisation' are often used as though there is a clear definition of what this means, but the reality is that there is a continuum of voluntary organisations, varying from very large charities with multi-million pound annual income and expenditure and a large paid workforce to small local voluntary groups run on a very small budget entirely by volunteers. Expenditure by voluntary organisations in Scotland alone in 2006-07 was £3.18 billion, of which nearly half was staffing costs (Scottish Government, 2009, p 4). Organisations in the third sector can be distinguished from the public sector healthcare authorities and local authorities in three main ways:

- they are set up independently of the state;
- they run themselves (that is, their governance is independent of the state);
- they rely at least to some extent on volunteers.

Some social enterprises blur this distinction between the state agencies and the third sector, since they share some characteristics of both the voluntary and private sectors. At its simplest, the voluntary organisation in the third sector does not distribute profits, whereas some social enterprises that straddle the boundary and possess some features of third sector organisations do distribute profits. In some parts of the UK, especially rural districts and communities that are isolated and dispersed as in Scotland, the notion of the 'social economy' is used (Scottish Government, 2009).

Local authorities have general performance standards and within different areas of health and social services there are national standards, referred to in the following chapters where appropriate. There are also arrangements made by the state to assure the quality of services. The Commission for Social Care Inspection (CSCI) was set up under the 2003 Health and Social Care (Community Health and Standards) Act and until 2009 was responsible for registering, inspecting and reporting on social care services in England. The Commission for Healthcare Audit and Inspection was set up in 2004 and became known as the Healthcare Commission (HCC). In 2009, both the CSCI and HCC were replaced by the Care Quality Commission (CQC).

Ofsted (formerly the government inspectorate of schools) inspects and regulates children's services in England and the CQC inspects adult services. Northern Ireland does not have an inspectorate for social care, this function being carried out by the Office of Social Services in the DHSSPS. In Wales, the Care and Social Services Inspectorate (CSSI) inspects and regulates the entire care system. The Social Work Inspection Agency in Scotland inspects and regulates all social care and the Scottish Education Inspectorate participates in joint inspections of children's services.

Regulating and assuring quality of services

In England there is a basic split between the regulation of standards of children's services and health and social care services. The CQC is the government body established under the 2003 Health and Social Care (Community Health and Standards) Act and is responsible for assuring the quality of health and social care services. Ofsted is responsible for inspecting all children's services, including social work, child protection and childcare, as well as early years services and schooling.

In Scotland, the Care Commission regulates the standards of social care services. In Wales, the DHSS is responsible for the Office of the Older People's Commissioner and the Office of the Children's Commissioner, as well as the Healthcare Inspectorate Wales (HIW) and the CSSI, both of which are independent of the Welsh Assembly Government (WAG) and report directly to the National Assembly for Wales (NAW). In Northern Ireland the Regulation and Quality Improvement Authority (RQIA) is the independent body responsible for regulating the standards of health and social care services; in contrast with England, this includes social services for children and adults. The DHSSPS in Northern Ireland launched quality standards for health and social care in 2006 (DHSSPS, 2006).

Social workers, laws and accountabilities

While it would be going too far to suggest that social workers undertake so many professional tasks that they require octopus tentacles to manage them all, it is nevertheless true that they do exercise responsibilities across a broad area of human experience. The professional identity of social workers rests, on the one hand, in their role as social care professionals and, on the other hand, as described in a key law text, as 'creations of statute working within the law' (Brayne and Carr, 2008, p 51). This means that, as we saw in Chapter One, social work has its roots in historical traditions of mutual aid and community development; the 21st-century profession of social work is not in existence primarily because of demands from clients for services, but is a creation of the state, largely because of certain laws that provide services for, and intervene in the lives of, children and adults, such as disabled, older or mentally ill people.

Legal system and social work

Social workers relate to the UK's legal system and it is important for them to understand enough about the law to make sure that their decisions and actions are lawful. Social workers are not lawyers, however – they use the law, but they are not professional legal practitioners. At the same time, social workers are more than just legal practitioners. They work with other people – professionals as well as the people who use social services and their carers – in interpreting and applying the law. So, while practising according to the law is an important part of social work, not every aspect of practice is covered by legal powers. Three important points need making here:

1. The legal system and the law are sites not of certainty and balance between competing interests in society, but of debate, controversy and constant change.
2. The laws on which social workers draw include those focusing on people's rights, challenging discrimination and advocating equality-based practice. Many of these are the outcome of campaigns partly fought on behalf of, and partly by, discriminated-against and socially excluded individuals and groups of people.
3. This body of empowering, rights-based legislation forms only a part of the laws that social workers use. They also rely on laws giving them and their employers duties, powers and responsibilities that they must exercise when intervening in the lives of children and adults, service users and carers.

Laws

The conduct of people's lives is governed by a system of laws that must be obeyed, and there are three main kinds of laws: **common law** handed down through tradition and accumulating and changing through precedent, which means the ever-growing body of case decisions made in court; **equity law**, which refers to the laws used in family law work, operated through the Courts of Chancery and, for instance, concerned with how goods are divided between separating couples; and **statute law**, which is laws passed by Parliament.

When social workers are undergoing qualifying programmes, they learn about the legal basis for practice. They are encouraged to read the statutes and become familiar with their content, so that they can work confidently with children and adults as well as with families, in their dealings with lawyers and the courts. The reality is that while social workers are not expected to act like lawyers, their professional opinion on how the law should be used is still valued by other professionals and valuable to the children and adults with whom they work.

Courts

The hierarchical arrangement of the court system in the UK can be thought of as rather like a family tree, much simplified in the accompanying figure (Figure 4.1). The different courts, through the judges presiding over them, apply statute laws by interpreting them, and draw on common law and equity as they feel appropriate.

Criminal proceedings are located in the first place in the Magistrates' Court and most cases (including **summary** offences, that is, the more minor offences) begin and end there. At the other end of the continuum, **indictable** offences (more major offences such as manslaughter and serious violence against the person) move quickly through the Magistrates' Court to the Crown Court, where they must be dealt with. In between are **either way** offences that may be dealt with in the Magistrates' Court or in the Crown Court. Civil Courts include the Magistrates' Court, County Court and High Court and civil proceedings include much of the professional business of social workers, including cases dealing with childcare, contact between children and separated or divorced parents and matrimonial cases. When Magistrates' Courts deal with family cases, they are called Family Proceedings Courts. The rules set out in legislation – under the 1989 Children Act, which applies largely in

Figure 4.1: Family tree of the UK courts and tribunals

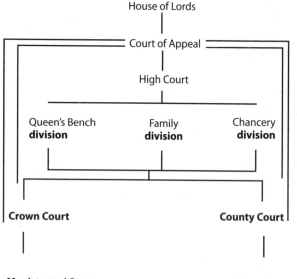

England and Wales and in some important aspects in Northern Ireland and Scotland – are the most likely ones to be followed by social workers.

Sometimes social workers work with **tribunals**, responsible for resolving disputes between person-to-person disputes and disputes between people and the state. A common tribunal is the Employment Tribunal that, as the title suggests, deals with disputes involving employee and employer, or the Care Standards Tribunal, which deals with appeals under the 2000 Care Standards Act 2000.

What this brief summary cannot convey is the complex interaction between the different courts, although Figure 4.1 does indicate some of the major points of connection. In practice, authority is exercised downwards through the family tree, as legislation and case precedents have an impact on services, while some cases and appeals can move upwards, for instance, as appeals from the lower courts are heard in higher courts. For the sake of clarity on Figure 4.1, only the links between the lower courts and the Court of Appeal are indicated, whereas in practice appeals to the High Court and the House of Lords may take place.

European and UK legislation

This brings us to an important complication of legislation, namely, how far European conventions (a convention can be thought of in this context as an agreement or treaty that to a greater or lesser extent is legally binding on those who are parties to it) and UK laws apply in the four countries of the UK.

The UK is subject, by and large, to much European legislation, as its four countries are members of the European Union (EU).This is something of a simplification, since not all European laws are accepted unconditionally by all member countries. Nevertheless, European laws are an important aspect of the impact of the EU on the UK, as exemplified in the 1950 European Convention on Human Rights (ECHR), which the British government signed up to in 1953. However, it was not until the passing of the Human Rights Act in Westminster in 1998 that the rights of citizens under the ECHR could be enforced through the UK courts (Brayne and Carr, 2008, p 73).

Increasingly, since the late 20th century, European laws have had an impact on legislation and practice in the UK. The 1998 Human Rights Act passed by the UK Parliament is a case in point, since it is affected to an extent by the ECHR, because the UK government has decided in general to comply with this European Convention, even though the government has discretion not to comply in particular aspects.

Within the UK, **devolution** is the term used to refer to the complex legal arrangements that preserve the separate legal system of Scotland and, under the 1998 Government of Wales Act, set up NAW and under the 2006 Government of Wales Act, empowers this Assembly to pass its own laws in areas such as local government, social services and social work.

Legal basis for services

In 1970 the Local Authority Social Services Act put the recommendations of the Seebohm Committee (Seebohm Report, 1968) into law, which led to the setting up of social services departments in England and Wales. In Scotland, social work departments were set up and in Northern Ireland health and social services were provided through regional boards.

These arrangements lasted nearly 30 years, until in the early 21st century the abolition of social services departments in England and Wales was accompanied by a clear split in the organisation of adults' and children's services in 150 local authorities. New departments of adult care services were set up and under the 2004 Children Act education and children's social care services were combined in new departments of children's services, which took up their responsibilities in 2007. Children's trusts and adult care trusts were set up, on similar lines to the NHS trusts which were already in place, delivering healthcare services.

Local authorities, through these trusts, were responsible for procuring and commissioning services for adults and children and their families. These arrangements had moved on considerably from the early 1990s, when under the 1990 NHS and Community Care Act what was called an internal market was set up, entailing a separation of the purchasing function from the provision of services. In effect, local authorities were required to reinvent themselves by contracting a minimum of four fifths of community care services from other provider agencies in the voluntary and private sectors. The providers of services could be a range of agencies, including the local authorities themselves, voluntary and private organisations. From the mid-1990s, under the 1996 Community Care (Direct Payments) Act, people receiving services could opt to receive direct payments from the local authority and purchase their own services, and from 2008 could hold personalised budgets comprising local authority funds and other resources, which meant that, in effect, they were commissioning and managing the provision of their own services. The principle of direct payments dates back nearly half a century, although they have only become more widely promoted by the government since the mid-1990s. In Scotland, local authorities were given advice in the 1968 Social Work (Scotland) Act on how to make direct payments and Section 7 of the 2002 Community Care and Health (Scotland) Act, encouraging the wider use of direct payments.

There has been a trend since the 1980s towards local authority services being contracted out to independent providers. The 1990 NHS and Community Care Act provided a new framework for social work as part of general health and social care services for people in the community and led to about 80% of social services for adults – from home care (domiciliary care such as meals on wheels) to residential care (such as residential homes for older people) – being provided by the private, voluntary and independent sector.

Before 1990, local authorities managed and provided the overwhelming majority of services, except in a few specialist areas such as the social work and residential services provided for children by large childcare charities (Barnardo's, The Children's Society and National Children's Homes), and services for older or disabled people provided by voluntary agencies such as the Leonard Cheshire Foundation. Twenty years on from this date, local authorities are the commissioners of services provided largely by agencies and organisations in the private, voluntary and independent sectors.

A selection of major legislation affecting social work and social care services is illustrated in Table 4.1.

Accountabilities, managerialism and discretion

We now consider three important and linked aspects of the relationship between social workers and the law, that together make their job more complex and demanding, but also more fascinating and potentially fulfilling: tensions arising from their multiple accountabilities; tensions between areas of their professional practice and control by managers; and tensions between their practice in clear-cut areas of the law and the discretion that they can exercise in some circumstances.

Table 4.1: Selected legislation related to social care and social work

1948 National Assistance Act	Duty of local authorities to provide residential and community care
1970 Local Authority (Social Security) Act	Duties of newly created social services departments
1983 Mental Health Act	Duty to appoint approved mental health professionals
1989 Children Act	Major enabling legislation for children
1990 NHS and Community Care Act	Sets out procedures for people's needs for community care to be assessed and services provided
1995 Disability Discrimination Act	Duty of local authority to prevent discrimination against disabled people through access to resources, buildings and services
1995 Carers (Recognition and Services) Act	Extends rights of carers to services
1996 Community Care (Direct Payments) Act	Social services department may provide cash to person, to enable them to purchase services
2000 Carers and Disabled Children Act	Carers needs can be assessed and they have a right to receive services, as carers
2000 Care Standards Act	Sets out framework for inspecting care and residential services
2004 Carers (Equal Opportunities) Act	Further extends rights of carers to services
2004 Children Act	Reforms children's services
2005 Mental Capacity Act	Specifies people's rights relative to their capacity
2006 Health and Social Care Act	Extends services for mothers of young children
2006 NHS and NHS (Wales) Act	Aftercare following hospital, services for people receiving mental health guardianship and home help services
2007 Mental Health Act	Updates mental health legislation over 25 years

Balancing tensions between multiple accountabilities

Social workers are accountable to many different sources of authority (see Figure 4.2) and this reflects the complexities of the personal, familial and community settings in which social work takes place. As social workers maintain a balance between competing interests and demands, they are, in effect, managing potential conflicts of interest that complicate decision making.

Figure 4.2: Multiple accountabilities of a social worker

Among the wide variety of accountabilities identified in Figure 4.2, there are two main strands:

- professionally, to their profession, to their own professional and personal values, to their professional colleagues and to their clients;
- managerially, to their managers and through them to their employing organisation.

These different accountabilities of social workers set up tensions which can erupt into visible conflicts, for instance, when choices need making and resources are scarce and managers propose putting agency priorities first and social work values suggest putting the person's needs first.

The complexities of different accountabilities identified above emphasises the requirement for social workers to balance their accountabilities to different sources of authority – legal, organisational, professional and personal – each of which embodies expectations and values which, to an extent, even though they overlap, are different. The diversity of these accountabilities is far wider, as Figure 4.2 shows. On occasions it may be difficult to reconcile these differences. We can add to this complex picture the diversity of people whose needs and wants (this useful distinction is between the 'needs' the professional may identify and the 'wants' expressed in the person's own wishes and choices) social workers are attempting to satisfy. These mean that social work cannot be reduced to a simple formula or set of procedures governing a limited number of situations. Social workers need to work responsibly and reliably, yet imaginatively and creatively, to manage this complexity. The first duty of the social worker should be to the wishes of the service user and the parent or carer, but within the family there may be conflicts of interest between children, young people and adults, between adult partners or ex-partners and between other adults in the family. In addition, the social worker has a responsibility to his or her own values and to professional values and those of colleagues in the team, yet is also employed to exercise the duties and powers of the service-providing agency, and to apply the law on behalf of the state. It is difficult, therefore, to arrive at a simple rule of practice.

Managing tensions between areas of professional practice and control by managers

Dustin's (2007) research shows how reorganisations of social services organisations in the UK from the early 1990s has led to the rise of managerialism. **Managerialism** is the term used to refer to circumstances in which being controlled (that is, conforming to, or complying with, the requirements and demands) by managers takes priority over professional responsibilities. A major consequence is that in adult care the provision of social care services ceases to be provided purely on the basis of a person's needs, but is subject to **commodification**, that is, becoming a commodity to be bought in a market where, regardless of demand (which may be high and rising) it is priced and bought and sold at that price, according to financial criteria rather than the intangible and human-led criteria of people's vulnerabilities and personal and social needs (Dustin, 2007, p 59).

Research into the basis of social workers' decision making indicates that there is a tension between satisfying one's accountability to professional social work values and goals and meeting the expectations of the employing organisation. There is a tendency for practitioners to experience stress and, where this happens, to focus on meeting the requirements of the organisation, losing the focus on using and developing professional expertise (McDonald et al, 2008; Sullivan, 2008).

Managing tensions between using the law and exercising discretion and judgement

Government is accountable to the general public for its work and it creates laws in order to carry out its work. Social workers are instruments of the government, in that they fulfil legal requirements in providing services for people and implement the law when on occasions they intervene in people's lives. Social workers are accountable to the government, through their employers, for the way they practise, within the framework of laws that dictates what they do. In some areas social workers exercise powers without any discretion, but in other areas they have wider discretion to choose how they practise.

So social workers do not simply use the law. In particular situations, while part of what social workers do is laid down in statute, part also lies within the practitioner's discretion. These statutes take different forms, categorised in one expert view (Braye and Preston-Shoot, 2009, p 92) as follows:

- Acts of Parliament: these prescribe the duties and powers of social workers
- regulations: these indicate in detail how duties and powers should be exercised

■ guidance: this is published by the government and feeds agency policy and practice
■ procedures: these are the agencies' guidelines on how employees should practise
■ courts: these interpret the law and build up case law.

Social workers continually rely on knowledge of key legislation concerning work with children, families and adults who are vulnerable by virtue of mental health problems, disability or old age. Social workers carry out duties on behalf of the local authority providing services, they exercise powers and fulfil responsibilities. Their practice depends on these three aspects: duties, powers and responsibilities.

Ethical principles for using the law in practice

The accountability of social workers derives in large part from their employers and their agency. Social workers are not autonomous professionals. They are employees of agencies and ultimately work for the state. Practice is based on a code of ethical practice. This code safeguards the rights of people who receive services and their carers. It also protects their confidentiality and respects their right to choose, direct and consent where appropriate to their treatment.

So the ethical principles that guide their practice cannot derive straightforwardly from the people with whom they work. Some important principles can be drawn out of these codes of practice: enabling the voice of service users to be influential; prioritising the wishes of people who are 'hard to reach' and 'seldom heard'; and challenging discrimination and promoting equality-based practice.

Enabling the voice of service users to be influential

Accountability to the public – and particularly to service users and carers – has been a growing preoccupation of government since the 1990s. Legal measures to enable people to make their views heard and their grievances acted on have strengthened measures taken to enable people to make their contribution. As a consequence, tribunals where people can formally register taking issue with a decision or situation and inquiries into shortcomings of services on occasions do take into account the views and experiences of people who use services. However, inquiries are not without their limitations. Many inquiries and investigations are held in private, even confidentially, and are not subject to the same procedural openness as the judicial inquiry where witnesses are legally bound to attend and give evidence. There are clearly laid out complaints procedures in public authorities, however, and after the internal channels have been exhausted, a complainant can take the matter to the local government ombudsman, or a child can complain to the children's commissioner. There is a children's commissioner in each country of the UK, although the powers of each vary from country to country and the English children's commissioner is by no means the most empowered. Also, there are some obvious barriers to a child being assertive and confident enough to carry a complaint, question or problem to such a person.

Prioritising the wishes of people who are 'hard to reach' and 'seldom heard'

It is crucial for the social worker to recognise people's diversity and take on board their unique experiences and expressed wishes when assessing their needs and making decisions. The span of diversity is constantly expanding in many communities. In many provincial towns in the UK, dozens of languages are spoken by school children and in London more than 300 languages are spoken in schools. Research demonstrates that the true extent, nature and significance of diversity among majority and minority communities in the UK may not be adequately recognised in work with different cultures, ethnic and faith communities (Institute of Community Cohesion, 2008). The consequences of diversity in communities include increased richness but also increased fragmentation. Social workers need to take on board the implications of these changes when working in such communities, in particular ensuring that people who are seldom heard can take advantage of the full range of resources and services to which they are entitled.

Challenging discrimination and promoting equality-based practice

A primary concern of social workers is to be alert to discrimination, whether on the grounds of gender, age, ethnicity or disability. An important distinction needs to be drawn between recognising diversity and acknowledging discrimination. Discrimination is unfair or unjust treatment on the grounds of real or perceived difference. Diversity is often only recognised in relation to minority ethnic groups, whereas in reality it is important to appreciate it in indigenous (this word is used here to refer to the population traditionally, long-term or already living in a locality, appreciating that this also can apply to minority communities) communities as well. Social workers need to be sensitive to the diversity within all communities and to have the resilience to resist one person's, or one group's, attempts to deny the legitimacy of another's experience and viewpoint. This poses a challenge for the practitioner, who cannot deny personal inheritance and values and must attempt to set these alongside values that will often conflict.

SUMMARY

This chapter has dealt with the relationship between the legal system, the law and social work. It has discussed the legal basis for social workers' use of powers, duties and responsibilities – their agency – and has examined how social work is organised. It has illustrated some of the ways in which social workers use the law, in recognition that, even though social workers are not lawyers, their detailed grasp of the law relating to children, families and adults places them well to make a uniquely well-informed contribution to decisions about people's welfare, needs, wishes and preferences.

RECOMMENDED READING

A sound examination of the perspectives and ideas around notions of ethical and accountable practice: Banks, S. (2006) *Ethics and values in social work* (3rd edn), Basingstoke: Palgrave.

Nearly 700 pages of authoritative reference material on key social work law: Brayne, H. and Carr, H. (2008) *Law for social workers* (10th edn), Oxford: Oxford University Press.

WEB LINKS

Information on the importance of the third sector:

National Council for Voluntary Organisations: coordinates voluntary organisations and provides information and resources
www.ncvo-vol.org.uk/

Office of the Third Sector, based in the Cabinet Office of the government, coordinating policy in the voluntary sector
www.cabinetoffice.gov.uk/third_sector/about_us.aspx

Volunteering England: coordinates organisations that use volunteers
www.volunteering.org.uk/

Part 2
Practising social work

5

social work with children, young people and their families

Introduction

This chapter deals with a key aspect of government policy – childcare and social work with children and families. Government policy since the end of the 20th century has located the quality of childcare and education near the heart of the goal of abolishing child poverty by 2020. Work with parents and the expansion of Early Years services were prioritised, with impetus given to provision for babies and very young children symbolised in the publication *Birth to three matters* (Sure Start Unit, 2002), and work with pre-school children, young children at primary school, children in mid-childhood and older children all receiving attention in many initiatives, brought together most notably in the publication of the government Green Paper *Every Child Matters* (DfES, 2003).

There is a general division in the UK between social care and social work services for children and families and those for adults. To some extent this has to be a somewhat artificial boundary, since in theory parents of children in need may receive services as carers for their children while receiving social care services as adults. These are matters that test the aim of government to deliver care, education, health, housing and social services that are well coordinated and tailored to the circumstances and needs of individuals. It is a distinctive feature of social work that practitioners are well placed to help this aspiration become a reality. Where there have been major shortcomings in children's services, the lack of effective joint working between different organisations and professionals has been identified repeatedly in inquiry reports (Reder and Duncan, 2004, p 98) as a problem. By the way, this is not to say that we should accept at face value the production of these inquiry reports. Butler and Drakeford (2006), through their critical analysis of particular aspects of the politics of these inquiries, raise our awareness that scandals and the inquiries that follow contribute to the public image of social work and are part of the mass media representation of social workers, but do not of themselves reflect everyday realities of practice.

Social work with a child is always undertaken with due regard to the child's family. It is important to bear in mind the centrality of the notion of the family in the UK, as in western societies in general. This is true, regardless of whether parents and other relatives are still living, or whether they are still in touch with each other or their children. Sometimes, even though the child's biological parents may not be significant to the child, there will be other adults acting as carers, or significant adults. So, whatever the child's circumstances social work with children tends to mean social work with children and their families or their carers.

Social workers often find themselves in settings where children and their families needing services are in touch with a range of agencies and it becomes crucial that practitioners act to ensure that decisions flow into well-connected practice.

Children, young people and their families receive services in England and Wales through children's services departments, set up in the first decade of the 21st century after the merger of former local authority education departments and divisions of children's services within the former social services departments. We can distinguish England and Wales, where most services for children and families are organised and managed separately from service for adults, from Scotland, where with some exceptions social work departments are responsible for the full range of services to children in need and their families, young people and adults, including child offenders.

Local authorities have legal duties to safeguard children and to ensure they are brought up free from risk of harm, healthy, educated and able to take a full part in their communities. Social work in this field carries significant responsibilities, offers the opportunity to develop specialist expertise in many major areas and provides challenging yet rewarding settings for work with children, young people, their parents and/or carers.

Contexts for practice

Changing families: constructing childhoods

Family structures and family members' lives are changing and childhood is as much a social construction as a biological fact. As society changes, so the structure of families, and the lives of family members, also change. The family in the UK, as in other western countries, has changed its forms in response to changing economic and social conditions. Bradshaw et al (2005, p 71) point out that the economic circumstances of the family are 'one of the single most important elements of a child's origins that affect their development and subsequent life chances'. Among these factors, differences of wealth and income are central, with babies born into the lowest social classes far more prone to illness and infant death than those born into the highest social classes.

Impact of inequalities of gender and power

Feminist theory and research from the 1960s has made a unique contribution to understanding the dynamics of family life and relationships between males and females in and out of the family, in particular highlighting imbalances of power between children and adults and men and women. Associated with these imbalances is the significant incidence of abuse and violence against women by men. Between March 2006 and March 2008, more than 144,000 males were prosecuted in the UK for offences of violence against women (CPS, 2009, p 2). The *UN Declaration on the Elimination of Violence Against Women*, (UN, 1993) defines violence against women as not just physical, sexual and economic, but as including psychological and emotional abuse such as threats and verbal behaviour, as well as acts of omission such as denial of access to nutrition, education and healthcare. Kapoor (2000) notes that violence against females can continue throughout the life cycle, from controlling decisions about abortion, through genital mutilation of girls, and involving girls and women in human trafficking and prostitution, to bringing about suicides and being involved in murder, more than one woman per week in the UK being murdered by her partner. In November 2009 the UK government announced that material on developing respectful, non-abusive and non-violent relationships and combating male violence against women would be incorporated as a compulsory component of the curriculum for school children of all ages (Travis, 2009).

Social responses to children as an intrinsically challenging 'problem'

In many western societies such as the UK, childhood in general and growing up through the 'terrible teens' or 'adolescence' in particular, are regarded by many people as intrinsically difficult and challenging for other adults in general and parents in particular. Other members of the community, for instance, often regard groups of young people on the street as a threat, simply by their presence and their different style of dress. Social workers, however, tend to become involved professionally in the lives of children and young people and their families, when their problems become sufficiently major to affect their own development or to threaten the well-being of others. This places social workers at the junction between children's and young people's experience and other people's (usually this means adults' rather unsympathetic) views of them. Social workers therefore have to manage this continual, uneasy and often irreconcilable divergence of views and experiences in their work with children and young people.

Childhood: socially constructed rather than a biological fact

The intrinsically problematic place of children in society forms part of a wider issue. Childhood is often said to be more of a social construction than a physiological series of stages through which all infants must expect to pass in a similar way on the journey to adulthood. In fact, in pre-industrial societies children experience very different childhoods to the modern, western industrialised childhood. In the rapidly growing industrial towns of Britain in the mid-19th century, for instance, working-class children were expected to labour in the factories and mills for long hours, alongside adults. Compulsory schooling only became law from 1870 and then only for children older than five and younger than 13, in England and Wales. Since then, children's developmental needs have been recognised by the state, with professionals in pre-school, primary and secondary education, as well as in health, leisure and youth services, providing for their needs from birth until adult hood.

It is important to make two general points about the context of practice, before going into the detail of different aspects of specialist work:

1. There has been a shifting preoccupation over recent years from intervention to preventive work. An increasing focus of social work is early prevention, that is, work with families identified as having children at risk, often children who are very young. It is possible to view this negatively, but on the other hand, as Parton (2006) notes, early intervention can be regarded as positive welfare, that is, justifying intervening early, before crisis situations arise.

2. There is a tension, reflected in all the policies, laws and practice relating to children, between different perspectives on childhood (see Figure 5.1).

Figure 5.1: Contrasting dimensions of childhood and views of children

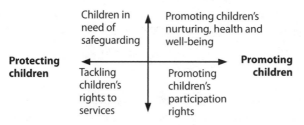

Welfare needs of children

Children in need of safeguarding

Promoting children's nurturing, health and well-being

Protecting children

Promoting children

Tackling children's rights to services

Promoting children's participation rights

Justice/rights of children

Protecting or promoting: welfare or justice

Policy, law and practice relating to children and young people since the second half of the 20th century has reflected a tension between meeting children's welfare needs and advancing their participation rights. Article 12 of the UN Convention on the Rights of the Child (UNCRC) promotes these and this is supported by the Welsh Assembly, but the English Parliament does not unreservedly adopt the UNCRC, holding back, for instance, on supporting children's rights not to be smacked and for offending children and the children of asylum seekers to be locked up in custodial settings. Nevertheless, campaigns continue for the rights of children; for instance, to raise the age of criminal responsibility (at which children can be prosecuted) from 10 years to 12 or even 14, so in keeping with other European countries. The campaigning organisation Children Are Unbeatable! campaigns for the UK to satisfy human rights obligations and protect children from assault on the same basis as adults (www.childrenareunbeatable.org.uk). A Welsh publication (WAG, 2004a, 2004b) advocates the rights of children to citizenship, with accompanying responsibilities and rights, whereas the English policy reflected in the adoption of the Green Paper *Every Child Matters* (DfES, 2003) emphasises the need of children for safeguarding and nurturing. Children's rights are currently promoted through the creation of children's commissioners in the four countries of the UK in the early 21st century, although England was slower than the other UK countries to appoint a commissioner and there is somewhat uneven progress of children's rights in different countries of the UK. The office for the children's commissioner for Wales, for instance, was created by the 2000 Care Standards Act.

Policy and local authority services

Since the second half of the 20th century, there has been growing recognition that children's later development depends on them having **secure attachments**, that is, positive, nurturing relationships with caring adults in parental roles, in their early years, partly as a means of strengthening their future **resilience**, that is, their ability to surmount negative experiences. Local authority services for children are both preventive (promoting good parenting, positive family experiences, education and health and well-being) and interventive (using the law to safeguard children from actual abuse or the risk of harm).

Legal basis for practice

The two major legal measures affecting the nature and delivery of services to children and families, apart from the 2000 Care Standards Act that dealt with the regulation and inspection of children's services, are the 1989 and 2004 Children Acts. Children's services were restructured in England and Wales after the 2004 Children Act, with the merger of education and social services for children and families and the creation of children's trusts in England and children and young people's partnerships in Wales. Children's trusts bring together all the services for children and young people in a locality, with a view to improving their outcomes. They develop children's trust arrangements, consisting of the local children and young people's partnership or similar body, with the duty of working together under the 2004 Children Act to plan and deliver joined-up services for the well-being of children and young people. This should entail maintaining an integrated strategy, integrated processes of joint planning and commissioning services from a range of agencies and organisations in the public, private, voluntary and independent sector, integrated processes of joint working and integrated delivery of practice organised around the child, young person and their family, rather than professionals working within the boundaries of existing agencies.

1989 Children Act

The 1989 Children Act establishes that in any decisions and actions by the court and professionals the welfare of the child must be the paramount consideration. This does not resolve a longstanding tension between attending to the welfare of the child and promoting the child's rights, and social workers have to balance these competing goals. Since the 1990s there has been increasing awareness of the vulnerability of some children and the risks of child abuse and a trend towards children being treated less as passive and dependent and more as active and articulate participants and contributors to decision making (James and James, 2004, pp 191-2). Social workers play a vital part in supporting children and although intervention is necessary in situations where they are being harmed or are at immediate risk of harm, preventive work can also be undertaken. Prevention includes a range of measures to safeguard the child and prevent dangers to health and well-being. Intervention becomes necessary at the point where the child's needs can only be met by action involving supervision of the situation of the child and family or, where no alternative is possible, removing the child from the family, either temporarily or on a permanent basis. This may entail living in a children's home or similar establishment, or being fostered (temporarily looked after) or adopted (permanently placed) by parents other than the child's biological parents.

With these factors in mind, the operation of the 1989 Children Act tends to reflect the principles of:

■ retracting and where possible minimising state interventions;
■ safeguarding children from harm and promoting their welfare;
■ taking the rights of children into account and ensuring they take part in decisions affecting them;
■ accepting that the best place for the child is the child's own family.

The measures in the Act support the notion that the local authority, on behalf of the state, should only intervene in cases where the threshold criteria are met. These threshold criteria include:

■ cause for concern that the child is suffering, harm, and/or is beyond parental control;
■ the notion of respecting the child and making sure that the views and wishes of the child are listened to;
■ supporting the welfare of the child;
■ minimising delay in the processing of the child's circumstances through the court;
■ that there should be no order by the court unless it would benefit the child more to have one;
■ the notion of clarifying what parental responsibility entails and when it applies. **Parental responsibility** is a term referring to the legal duties, rights, powers and responsibilities of a parent in relation to

a child under legislation which includes the 1989 Children Act and later legislation, the 2002 Adoption and Children Act, ensuring that unmarried mothers and fathers can exercise continuing parental responsibility.

The 1989 Children Act contains the **welfare checklist** (summarised in Table 5.1), which is a list of items to be considered by a court in a dispute involving any child.

Table 5.1: **Welfare checklist**
The court needs to consider:
the wishes and feelings of the child, taking into account the child's age and understanding
the physical, educational and emotional needs of the child
the likely consequences for the child of any change in the child's situation
nature of relevant characteristics of the child, such as age, gender, background
harm, or risk of harm, to the child
capacity of the child's parents, or other significant adults in the view of the court
the available powers of the court

The duties of the local authority, carried out, on the whole, by social workers, include:

- identifying children who are in need;
- assessing children in need;
- making sure that children in need receive services to meet their needs;
- preventing abuse and neglect and in this way reducing the requirement for care proceedings to take place;
- registering children who have physical impairments or learning disabilities.

Safeguarding children

Children are affected traumatically by violence. Research by the UN (2006) estimates from accounts given by children and young people themselves that in a typical city of 100,000 children – that is, bigger than Hull but smaller than Leeds – one child under the age of 15 will be murdered each day, usually by a parent; over a third of the children will be hit by their parents; up to 10,000 children will be sexually abused at some point while they are growing up; and because of this, or other, abuse, violence or neglect, 240 children will become subject to a child protection plan.

Since the 1989 Children Act, the term **safeguarding children** has become placed at the forefront of social work with children. Before this, a succession of scandals took place, from the 1940s (Curtis Committee, 1946), some of which contributed directly to attempts to reform and improve childcare policy and practice. By the early 21st century, much of the professional territory of safeguarding children who have been abused, or who are at risk of abuse, has become public through the concern of the mass media and the general public over the specific cases of children who have been seriously harmed or killed. The inquiry into the unlawful death of Victoria Climbié conducted by Lord Laming (Laming, 2003) made many recommendations and led to the government Green Paper *Every Child Matters* (DfES, 2003). Children's safeguarding boards were set up, linked with a wider strategy of improving the coordination, and in some settings, integration of children's services. The unlawful death of Baby Peter in 2008 rekindled public, professional and political concerns about continued shortcomings in child protection in the UK. Lord Laming (2009) wrote a follow-up report on his earlier work, recommending improved training for social workers, better support for their practice and additional measures to safeguard children. A government task force was set up with the aim of identifying remedies for the shortcomings of social work.

2004 Children Act

The 2004 Children Act supplements and complements the 1989 Children Act without replacing it. Five main desirable outcomes for children have been developed as part of the policy and practice initiatives that followed the 2004 Children Act, under the umbrella heading of Every Child Matters:

- Stay safe
- Be healthy
- Enjoy and achieve
- Sustain economic well-being
- Make a positive contribution to society.

Social workers share responsibility with other professionals in health and social care, social services and children's services for promoting children's and young people's health and well-being. The National Service Framework (DfES and DH, 2004) establishes national standards to promote children's and young people's health and well-being, and there are 11 standards:

- Standard 1: identifying needs and early intervention, through the Child Health Promotion Programme led by the NHS in partnership with local authorities.

The other 10 standards include:

- support for parents;
- family-centred services for children and young people;
- safeguarding and promoting the welfare of children and young people;
- ill children and young people;
- children and young people in hospital;
- children and young people with disabilities and with complex health needs;
- children's and young people's mental health and psychological well-being;
- medicines for children and young people;
- maternity services.

Health improvement for children and young people depends on their active participation and empowerment, by

- giving them information about the issues;
- encouraging them to develop opinions;
- offering opportunities to tell decision makers what they think;
- providing feedback as to how their opinions have shaped services;
- ensuring ways are found of taking account of the views of children and young people from a diversity of ages, abilities, cultures and backgrounds.

Social work takes place with the diversity and complexity of children's needs

It is increasingly recognised that all children are different and this diversity makes the task of working effectively with them to meet their needs complex and demanding (James and James, 2004, p 13). Social workers often engage with children who are excluded from other services, such as the children of asylum seekers, refugees and travellers. Older children and young people who have problems of illegal drug and alcohol consumption, or girls who become pregnant before they have the capacity to bring up a child themselves, may also become part of the caseload of social workers. Social workers may also work with children suffering from life-threatening illnesses which lead to impairments, and which affect their family life. Social workers tend to be called into such situations when the problems become multiple and the task of responding to them is complex.

Risk and harm: prevention or intervention?

The notion of threat, or risk as it is most widely known in social work, underlies two categories of work – intervention and prevention. Intervention takes place when a problem has already become visible; prevention is, as it sounds, work aiming to prevent problems becoming worse, or arising in the first place.

Critics of social work services may argue that problems affecting children should be 'nipped in the bud', which implies that young children, in particular, can be assessed in their family settings and future risks of problems avoided through preventive social work. One simple barrier to this exists: while in general much is known about the kinds of family circumstances which may contribute to problems in older childhood, or even in adulthood, in circumstances where many children experience disturbances of one kind or another in their childhoods, no techniques or tools exist to ensure certain prediction of which children and adults will experience problems, unless professional intervention takes place. This is why social work, psychology, psychiatry and many therapies are often regarded as closer to the arts than to the sciences.

Social workers take a lead responsibility for ensuring that local authorities use the least restrictive and least harmful options when working with children and their families. This means that wherever possible, social workers will

- prevent children coming into care;
- if children come into care, work intensively to reduce the time they spend in care;
- when children reach the point of leaving care, ensure this transition is made as smoothly, supportively and positively as possible.

Settings for practice

Social work is practised with children in many settings, both formal and informal. That is to say, social work with children may take place anywhere – at home, in the school playground, in residential, foster care and adoption, or in a children's centre. Children's centres grew out of the Sure Start programme, in the sense that the government decided to extend them in the light of the experience of Sure Start.

Sure Start local programmes (SSLPs) began in 1999 with the aim of providing additional family support to reduce the impact of social exclusion on young children and their families who lived in deprived localities. After 2005, children's centres progressively replaced the original

Sure Start centres. Research indicates that in general, children benefit from SSLPs and that the main reason for this lies in the improved quality of parenting (Belsky et al, 2007). Social workers play a crucial part in helping families whose children and young people are learning disabled, or who have mental health or drug or alcohol misuse problems, to gain access to services.

Approaches to practice
Principles of practice

The practice of social work with children and families is holistic, child-centred and guided by the welfare principles of the 1989 Children Act expressed in the welfare checklist (see Table 5.1). **Holistic** practice is a term that means taking into account a view of the child as a complete person in his or her family and environment. Thus, the social worker, in assessing the child, reaches a view together with the child and the parents or carers that takes into account the entirety of the child's needs, in the context of the family and the wider social setting including such aspects as the extent of social exclusion, quality of housing and support and resources available in the local community.

It is vital that practice is child-centred, not just in the sense that listening to children is important (McLeod, 2007, p 278), but also that their rights should be upheld. The scope of child-centred practice can be represented in a diagram (see Figure 5.2).

Social work with children and families entails a great range of approaches, from therapeutic work, group work and a range of preventive approaches. Sometimes it will be necessary for health and children's services to reach out to therapeutic or health – including complementary therapies – services as part of the plan to meet the child's needs, as the following example shows.

Figure 5.2: **Child-centred practice**

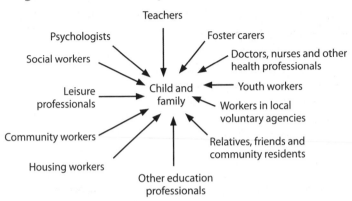

Example

Carla is six and has been diagnosed as asthmatic. She has suffered intermittently from eczema since infancy. Medication has failed to control these worsening problems. Carla's social worker has supported Carla's lone-parent mother, who suffers from mental health problems of depression, related to trying to manage her debt problems through low-paid part-time or unsocial work, ie. work carried out in unsocial conditions or at unsocial times.

The social worker refers Carla through the multidisciplinary children and families team to the local holistic healthcare practice, based in the health centre run by the primary care trust (PCT). After six months of homeopathic treatment by a general practitioner (GP) who is also a registered homeopath (non-doctors can only practise as lay homeopaths), Carla's symptoms have abated and are assessed as under control.

Key stages of practice with children and families

Social workers have a central role in working with children and families, through the key stages of

- investigating
- carrying out an initial assessment
- carrying out a core assessment
- planning services in consultation with children and their families
- intervening and implementing services
- reviewing and evaluating services.

Social workers are equipped with knowledge and understanding of key legislation when carrying out such work. The 1989 Children Act tends to be referred to a good deal because it specifies the responsibilities of statutory local authority departments and partner agencies in areas such as:

- the duty to investigate and hold strategy meetings (Section 47);
- application for a Child Assessment Order (Section 43);
- Emergency Protection Order (Section 44);
- police protection (Section 46);
- different supervision orders (Sections 31-5).

Practice

The process of practice is governed by an **integrated children's system** which aims to achieve an integrated approach to the sequence of assessment, planning, intervening, reviewing and evaluating practice, as well as recording this systematically using information technology (IT). Despite this integrated approach, it is mainly safeguarding and investigating work in relation to child abuse and protection that attracts most public attention, and it is true that social workers with children and families do collectively have major lead responsibilities in this area. Social workers are responsible for investigating, for instance, in circumstances where there is an allegation of abuse against a child.

Pen picture

In the case of a fictional family, Hardy, for instance, the local authority employs the social worker to investigate on the basis of information received in a letter from the family's nanny. This has given reasonable cause for concern that Mr and Mrs Hardy, who give the impression of being a respectable middle-class couple, have caused their child significant harm. The investigation is carried out as a Section 47 inquiry under the 1989 Children Act. Despite protestations from the parents, the social worker must insist on seeing the child, Gemma aged six, and speaking to her. The social worker completes the welfare checklist when carrying out the inquiry report. This is later used in court as part of the supporting evidence.

Investigatory social work is not carried out in relaxed settings where relationships with family members are smooth and supportive. The role of investigator is inherently interventionist. It is vital that in such circumstances the social worker adopts an inquiring approach, what Laming (2009) calls a 'sceptical stance'. This enables the social worker to regard situations critically and to not accept at face value, but be ready to question what parents and carers say about the situation. It is essential that the investigating social worker separately sees and talks to family members, including partners and carers and each child in the household.

Pen picture (continued)

The preliminary investigation is complete. The social worker's inquiry leads to a joint strategy meeting with team colleagues to decide what should happen. Gemma is judged to be at risk of imminent harm. It is possible that further, more detailed inquiry will be carried out, but intervention is necessary first, to protect Gemma.

What short-term and long-terms orders are available to safeguard her? The following are the main options the social worker needs to consider, in consultation with colleagues. These are important options, with serious implications for family members, and decisions should be considered carefully. The police can remove Gemma now, if she is judged to be in immediate danger, and use police protection powers to remove her, or keep her in a place of safety for 72 hours. Children's services can take out any of the following orders under the Children Act 1989:

- Emergency Protection Order– an order granted under s.44, enabling the local authority of another authorised person to remove the child to a place of safety for a short period.
- Assessment Order – an order under s.43, requiring the child's development and health to be assessed.
- Supervision Order – an order under s.35, placing the child under the supervision of a social worker or probation officer.
- Interim Care Order – an order under s.38, committing the child to the care of the local authority for a limited period of eight weeks or less, subject to review.
- Care Order – an order under s.33 committing the child to the long-term care of the local authority.
- Residence Order – an order to live with a person under s.8, or under s.10(4) or s.5 – and potentially made either by the child's parent/s or any person the child has lived with recently for at least three years – for a residence order that discharges a care order.

Professional social workers go through a structured sequence in working with children and families: initial and core assessment, planning, implementation and evaluation.

Initial assessment

In many cases, the social worker will make an initial assessment of the situation and decide that the best action at this stage is no action. This follows a principle of the 1989 Children Act, often referred to as the 'no order' principle. The idea is that where possible parents and carers should be left to bring up their children without legal intervention by the authorities.

Core assessment

The aim is to achieve **integrated assessment**. The purpose of the core assessment is to enable a judgement to be reached about safeguarding and promoting the welfare of the child. A core assessment may be required for each child in the family. Among factors that need to be considered in a core assessment are the

- views and wishes of the child;
- views of the parents or carers – this is part of what is generally called 'working in partnership with parents';
- level of development of the child;
- extent to which the child has comprehension of the decisions and issues;
- time constraints;
- likelihood of making meaningful contact with the child;
- chance of finding an advocate for the mother so that she remains involved (for instance, where care proceedings take place through the court).

Initial assessment may result in the finding that there is a likelihood or evidence of significant harm to the child, in which case procedures will be followed for safeguarding children, including convening a Child Protection Conference within a short period of time and convening a core group to carry out a core assessment. The conference should normally take place within 15 days of the most recent strategy discussion. A core group will normally be organised within 10 days of the conference, comprising agencies and people working with the family.

A core assessment takes time to prepare (35 days may be allowed) and is a major social work task, although there are contributions from a range of agencies, not just children's services. When carrying out a core assessment the social worker is usually drawing on knowledge and understanding of child development and what is called an 'ecological approach' see below. Government guidance on the holistic assessment of the needs of children and families (DH, 2000) takes this approach, emphasising three components of the child's circumstances: the child's developmental needs; the parenting capacity of parents and carers; and family and wider environmental factors.

The child's developmental needs include: the child's self-care skills, education, health, emotional and behavioural development, and family and social relationships. The parenting capacity of the parents includes: their ability to provide basic care, ensuring safety, providing emotional warmth and stimulation, providing stability, guidance and maintaining boundaries. Family and environmental factors include: family history and functioning, the wider family, employment, housing, family income, the extent of the social integration of the family and community resources.

Approaches taking into account wider environmental factors are known as ecological. They add important richness to the assessment of the child, going beyond the parents and carers to the family's circumstances, in the wider setting of the community and society. It is important for wider environmental factors to be taken into account that may affect the child directly or indirectly, including

- the place of the child in the home, school and neighbourhood;
- how these relate to each other;
- the impact of settings in which the child does not take part, such as other family members' workplaces;
- the wider context of cultures and beliefs.

Two particular criticisms can be made of the assessment framework:

1. It tends to concentrate on assessing the deficits of children and their parents or carers, rather than building on their strengths.

2. It can simply be used by agencies to reinforce existing agency criteria for the eligibility of people for services, rather than responding to their needs. Research shows that some local authorities apply eligibility criteria strictly and that these often restrict their capacity to meet the full needs of children, especially children with physical impairments or learning disabilities, most children actually being eligible for services under the 1989 Children Act (Morris, 1998).

Planning services

The planning stage is crucial, since the success of future work depends on a realistic action plan which does not just meet the local authority's and the social worker's expectations, but also meets the goals of children and parents.

Pen picture

Alix is a lone parent and her son Marc is aged seven. The social worker has concerns that Marc's estranged father is threatening to take him to live with him and Marc is showing signs of abuse after the last contact with his father. The social worker recommends to her team leader that the local authority initiates a Section 47 investigation and it is agreed in the child protection team that a core assessment is undertaken.

Marc has been attending the local primary school and doing well. Under the subsequent action plan, the school and social workers work together to set new, shared outcomes and a transition plan, to ensure that Marc's progress is not affected adversely, should he have to move to live out of the immediate catchment area of the school.

When we consider the principle of consulting children, we need to appreciate its implications. It implies that children are able to express their choices and preferences. Social workers are expected to give children **informed choice**, which means that they are given enough information to enable them to consider all the options and possible outcomes, before making their choice. Research by Turner (2003) concludes that most of the preferences of disabled children are denied, despite the fact that, like any one else, they have preferences.

Implementation

Writing reports and giving evidence in court

The social worker is likely to spend a significant amount of time writing reports, as the outcome, for instance, of investigations, initial and core assessments. The social worker, on occasions, gives evidence in court and is cross-questioned by barristers on statements made in the reports. Each statement needs to be backed up by supporting evidence, and the social worker must give this information straightforwardly when asked.

Regarding the circumstances of the child and family, the social worker considers

- the wishes of the child, if these can be ascertained (the child may be too young to give a view);
- the risk to the child of significant harm;
- the likely effects on the child of any change in circumstances;
- whether the parents can provide care;
- the physical, educational and emotional needs of the child;
- the age, gender, ethnicity, culture and disability of the child;
- the nature of any powers available to the court.

Supporting children and families

The outcomes for children looked after by local authorities in the UK, particularly for children in residential care or those moved repeatedly through multiple residential and foster care placements, has historically not been good. Their performance in schools and in further and higher education has suffered. Research (see Fletcher-Campbell and Archer,

2003, p 1) found that of the total of care leavers, nearly half were not entered for GCSE or GNVQ at Key Stage 4, in contrast with the national average of less than 4% of children. Often, leaving care at 18 when, in legal terms, they become adults, has been a traumatic process. For social workers, improving these and other outcomes for children and families involves a multiagency organisational approach and a complex process of multidisciplinary practice.

Pen picture

Ahmed is 17 and, with the support of his social worker (a member of the looked-after children team of children's services), has been looked after since he was taken into care five years ago. His social worker is working with him under the 2000 Children Leaving Care Act. The local authority acts as 'corporate parent' for Ahmed and has introduced a corporate parenting strategy, which was developed with a group of parents and children in the authority and involves children and parents in continuing to improve services, support and the quality of parenting. This, his social worker anticipates, should enable him to make the transition to sixth form college and, Ahmed hopes as well, university. Ahmed's social worker is aware that children's services may work with him in this case until he has finished higher education in his early twenties.

A significant part of the work of more experienced and, where appropriate, post-qualified social workers involves intervention work and advocacy, or legal representation of children (Brayne and Carr, 2008, p 149). Clearly, while social workers are not trained lawyers, it is important that they know enough law to be able to fulfil their unique potential role as advocates for children and families, and, on occasions, as interveners in the lives of children and families.

Promoting health and well-being

Promoting the health and well-being of children is one of the goals of government policy under the banner of the Every Child Matters policy and practice initiative in the early 21st century. Social workers may need to tackle problems of obesity, by working with children and families, rather than by intervening as though obesity is simply a matter of parental neglect or abuse. Underweight, neglected children as well as overweight and perhaps pampered children should not automatically be treated similarly. Obesity is much more likely to be a public health issue. Social workers and health professionals are all likely to experience great difficulty in coming up with simple prescriptions to 'cure' obesity, which remains a complex problem and an issue that persists through childhood into adulthood.

Dealing with Dying and Bereavement in the Child's World

Death is not restricted to old age. Some children experience life-threatening diseases and conditions and some children experience the death of another child or adult friend or family member. Social workers may need to help children understand dying and death, including helping them realise that death cannot be reversed and is universal. Older children experience bereavement and respond to it differently to very young children, and social workers need to be able to work with them through these situations. Sometimes the death of one or both parents leads to children being taken into care, that is, being 'looked after' by the local authority, and this is an additional trauma with which these children have to cope. Children may need to talk to somebody and volunteers can be a valuable resource. They may help children to create ways of retaining memories, perhaps through a photograph album or memory box or through commemorating anniversaries and birthdays.

Dealing with Drug and alcohol problems

Since the 1990s, problems of young people using illegal drugs and drinking alcohol to excess have grown significantly. Increasing numbers have been engaged in treatment, including more than 60,000 illegal drug takers in 2007/08 who remained in structured treatment programmes for more than 12 weeks (see www.nta.nhs.uk/news_events/newsarticle. aspx?NewsarticleID=50).

Alcohol and illegal drug use affect adults as well, so some of them, as parents, put at risk of harm or neglect the children in their care.

While there is no consensus about the extent to which policies and laws should forbid illegal drug taking and restrict the use of alcohol to young people and adults, there is no doubt that the increasing availability of cheap hard drugs such as heroin, and the widespread advertising and availability of cheap alcohol through supermarkets, have exacerbated problems of substance misuse.

Social workers work with people who misuse drugs and alcohol to help them tackle their habit. The government's drug strategy is led by the National Treatment Agency for Substance Misuse (NTA) (www.nta.nhs. uk), the aim of which is to treat a person's habit, with the associated improvements brought about in their health, stability and reduced incidence of criminal activity. Social workers also work with the problems that arise as a consequence of substance misuse. Babies may be born who are already addicted to heroin. Children may be living in a house where other family members including parents are taking drugs. Alcohol misuse may be associated with criminal violence in the home (also known as domestic violence, a term which actually seems to domesticate it and play down its criminality).

Working with Refugees and asylum seekers

Refugees and asylum seekers have been housed in different communities throughout the UK, and social workers are likely to work with adults with children whose applications for asylum are being processed, those who have had their applications approved and those who are awaiting deportation, having had their applications refused. These very different circumstances generate very different issues for applicants and social workers need to be equipped to work with them, sometimes in situations of great stress and uncertainty. Some social work is practised in the vicinity of ports and airports.

Pen picture

Megan is one of the social workers in the asylum service operating in Aerotown, a local authority containing a major UK airport. The team work with children and families arriving at the airport. Megan specialises in work with children, from birth to 16. Other workers specialise in work with older age groups.

More than half a dozen children arrive every week and are referred by airport staff to the asylum service. Neeta is a 15-year-old who arrived yesterday. Megan and her colleagues follow their routine of carrying out an assessment to establish whether Neeta is trafficked or is an unaccompanied minor. Megan is aware that Neeta may have been badly treated before her journey or during it and may be traumatised now. The emphasis of Megan's work is on providing a rapid, efficient service and remaining sensitive to the needs and wishes of children and their families throughout.

Source: Based on a description of real practice (Sale, 2008, pp 20-1)

Intervention or prevention

Teams of social workers with children and families have often been likened to the fire brigade, rushing to deal with crises on an emergency basis. There the comparison breaks down, because at least the fire brigade, one way or another, remain engaged in the situation until the fire has been extinguished. Increasingly, fire brigades are involved in educating the public in how to prevent fires occurring in the first place.

Unfortunately, most of social workers' resources with children and families are devoted not to helping families prevent problems occurring, but to intervening in families where harm and abuse have already taken place. Furthermore, the focus is on investigating abuse, rather than on providing subsequent therapeutic and developmental support to children and families in the longer term. There is a major opportunity for the current and upcoming generations of social workers to develop preventive work with children and families, and to develop specialist therapeutic expertise at post-qualifying level.

Work with poverty and social exclusion

Domestic violence between adults (most commonly it is men who are violent towards their female partners) knows no boundaries of wealth or social class and can occur in any part of society. In contrast, most of the child protection work of social workers – where there is abuse or neglect – takes place with poorer families.

Family support and improving parenting

The government, through the Cabinet Office Social Exclusion Task Force, launched a families at-risk review in 2007 into how to reach and support an estimated 140,000 families at risk, who were judged to need increased family-tailored support at critical moments of family life (Social Exclusion Task Force, 2007). These at-risk families displayed five or more indicators of social exclusion, including

- poor housing
- nobody in the household in work
- family income 60% below the median (the middle income of a list from highest to lowest incomes)
- parents with no qualifications
- mother with mental health problems.

The government proposed a two-pronged approach to improving family life for children in these 'families at risk': better family support and measures to improve parenting. The Department for Children, Schools and Families (DCSF) devised better family support through intensive measures geared to family needs, through measures such as the Family Intervention Projects and their associated Family Intervention Panels. Principles of Family Intervention Projects include

- ensuring the family's needs are viewed holistically and not in separate boxes (that is, not one category for housing, one for employment and so on);
- ensuring adult family members are regarded by professionals as adults with children, that is, as parents;
- building on family strengths;
- tailoring the support and services provided specifically to family needs.

Pen picture

Megan is a social worker coordinating services for the Harper family, who are receiving support through the Family Intervention Panel in the borough. This provides the family with a range of intensive family support resources, including a range of different services from professionals working with three children aged under five, three teenagers and the lone-parent mother with her new partner. Work is being done to help the teenage daughter, aged 13, who has recently had an abortion, one son aged 14, who has been binge drinking and the other son aged 15, who has been excluded from school and is engaged in an anger management programme as a consequence of his recent court appearance. Megan works with teachers at the school to re-engage the son in school. In the process, teachers and the social worker each find out more about others' roles and learn to work more closely together.

The development of integrated approaches to education and social work professionals working together with children and families is a process of mutual learning, which can lead to increased effectiveness. Here is an example of preventive, community-wide work with children and families in a locality.

Pen picture

Help Ourselves (fictional name) is a local action group run by children and young people. It has organised a play scheme for themselves and for other children and young people, funded by local community efforts in partnership with the local authority. Help Ourselves is supported by a social worker in the local children and families team of children's services, who facilitates their meetings and activities, without usurping the leadership by children and young people.

Safeguarding children

The UK, like many other western countries, has a state-regulated system for protecting children from harm that has developed relatively recently, since the 1970s. This is multiprofessional, involving the police, doctors, nurses, teachers, lawyers and judges, but it is social workers who play the leading role in investigating incidents, intervening in families and removing children where necessary from their parents or carers.

Pen picture

Anik, 15, ran away from home about 12 months ago and is currently living with foster parents. She revealed that her stepfather was sexually abusing her and he is now serving a prison sentence. Her mother blames her for reporting him and thereby removing the father figure from their household and Anik is no longer welcome at home. Anik's social worker is working with her to reconcile her and her mother, while enabling Anik to complete her schooling and achieve her further aim of becoming a nurse.

The Children and Family Court Advisory and Support Service (CAFCASS) replaced the former Family Court Welfare Service (FCWO), created under the 2000 Criminal Justice and Court Services Act, to safeguard the welfare of children, advise courts, provide for children to be represented in family proceedings (that is, in court) and inform, advise and support children and families involved in such proceedings.

Working with homeless young people

Robinson (2008) shows the importance of this neglected area of practice. Homelessness has been recognised by government as a major social problem since the early 1970s when statistics first began to be gathered about numbers of homeless people (Robinson, 2008, p 15). The numbers of homeless people in general are regarded by professionals in the field as liable to be under-reported by local authorities (Robinson, 2008, p 19). There may be as many as 400,000 people in the UK in the total of 'hidden' homelessness. An unknown number of young people are homeless at any time, due to the fact that official statistics do not contain a separate category for them (Robinson, 2008, p 15).

Every year about 100,000 children and young people in the UK run away from home or from care. In 2009, the government established a *Young runaways action plan* (DCSF, 2009).

Pen picture

Abdul, 17, ran away from his home in a provincial town and was found by a volunteer working for a children's charity, living rough in London. He is living with foster parents. His social worker is trying to make contact with his family and ascertain what caused him to run away, with the aim of working with him towards an assessment of his present situation and a plan for the future, whether back with his family or living independently.

Social workers in schools

Since the 1960s when Sir Alec Clegg, chief education officer in the then West Riding of Yorkshire, introduced full-time social workers to schools (Clegg and Megson, 1968), to varying extents social workers have been associated with schools throughout the UK. In the integrated children's services of England and Wales, there are increasing opportunities for schools to become an important focus through which children and parents are able to gain quick and easy access to specialist services.

There is a need, however, to ensure that this trend does not also lead to other professionals in schools, such as teachers and counsellors, relying on social workers to deal with problems that should be dealt with by educational professionals. This implies that all professionals in schools, including social workers, clarify the nature of the various problems of pupils and define how they are assessed and responded to.

Working with children with special needs

Children may suffer from problems on the autistic and Asperger's syndrome spectrums. These children are often subject in schools to inclusion policies and practices, that is, strategies to include them in mainstream education. However, teachers and social workers may find themselves debating whether including children in the mainstream is advisable in every case since, increasingly in the early 21st century, professionals have advanced arguments for some children's special educational and social needs still to be met through highly supportive, non-stigmatising, yet segregated facilities and services.

Children may suffer from attention-deficit hyperactivity disorder (ADHD). Children with ADHD display persistent inattention, impulsivity and unnecessary or unwanted motor activity. Terms such as 'hyperactivity' and 'bad behaviour' are often used to refer to aspects of ADHD and some people reject it as a syndrome in the same way as dyslexia was a contested concept for many decades.

It is difficult to gather data on the incidence of ADHD, but the likelihood is that it affects about 5% of the child population, which approximates to an average of one or two children per class size of 30. The incidence of ADHD is higher in parts of the population where poverty and social deprivation are greater, which means that it often compounds other difficulties children experience as they grow up. ADHD often affects not only the child's learning at school, but also other aspects of personal, social and home life. It is more likely that children with ADHD will become drawn into deviant, aggressive and criminal activity than other children.

Social work with children with ADHD in one sense is an extension of good parenting. The social worker should reinforce the efforts of the parents to understand and be sensitive to the child's experience and feelings. ADHD makes demands on both children and parents and the social worker needs to ensure that sufficient support and services are available in all aspects of the child's life – at home, in school and in social and leisure activities. Parents, of course, will need support in all of these. Teachers will also need support and there are issues about whether it is preferable for the child with ADHD to be included in the mainstream of school timetabling and social and sporting activities. It is likely that the perspectives of teachers, the child with ADHD, the child's parents, other children and other professionals will differ on this.

It is clear that social work with children with ADHD is a multiprofessional activity which engages parents and children in a multidimensional way, in terms of the child's private, inner world of emotions and thoughts, as well as in family life, and the child's engagement in education, sporting, social and other leisure activities.

Pen picture

Gill and Joe are sister and brother aged 12 and 14 respectively, who are autistic. They live in a residential setting. Their social worker ensures that their care treatment and management plan entails them seeing a lot of their parents and working towards achieving independent living and living to their full potential, including developing their educational achievement, vocational skills, interests and leisure activities.

Key issues

Social workers: sceptical advocates

We need to remind ourselves of the necessity for practitioners to be both sceptical and advocates. There is a tension between these, just as there is a need to balance advocacy for children against scepticism of adults, as the potential abusers of children.

Sceptical: the inquiries subsequent to the death of Baby Peter confirm the need not just for an adherence to the research basis for practice, but also for what Lord Laming referred to in a radio interview on his report as an 'informed scepticism' by practitioners. This is a reminder of the need for practitioners to continuously subject to critical scrutiny what they are told about children by adults.

Advocates: social workers need to advocate for children. This means being sensitive and friendly towards children and respecting their vulnerability but also helping them to assert their views and rights.

Consulting children and children's rights

Social workers have a role to play in strengthening children's power to speak up for themselves and to state their own needs. It can be argued that society is over-punitive towards children. While on the one hand some children and young people are exploited – sexually and through child labour – others are brought up outside their natural home or, if child offenders or asylum seekers, may be locked up in institutions.

Children are still not protected from physical punishment by parents, which is still legal in the UK.

Whatever our personal views about the treatment of children, it is undeniable that some vulnerable children need advocates to champion their rights – rights to the basics of shelter, warmth, adequate food, nurturing and loving care, as well as to the higher needs for education, play and a happy home life with a reasonable prospect of personal and social fulfilment as they grow towards adulthood. Social workers can play a significant part in ensuring that these are not just pious hopes but become part of realistic planning and service provision for children in need.

SUMMARY

This chapter has provided an overview of social work with children, young people and families. This is a major area and dominant in social work, since it covers a huge variety of human problems. Social workers often specialise in different aspects of this work, which range from prevention, including safeguarding children and young people from the risks of abuse and harm, to intervention, with the aim of promoting the welfare of children and young people.

RECOMMENDED READING

An important source on standards of practice: DfES (Department for Education and Skills) and DH (Department of Health) (2004) *National Service Framework for children, young people and maternity services*, London: The Stationery Office.

A useful chapter covering practice issues regarding children and young people: Pike, S. and Forster, D. (1997) *Health promotion for all*, Edinburgh: Churchill Livingstone, pp 125-40.

WEB LINKS

Action on Addiction
www.actiononaddiction.org.uk

Addiction Dependency Solutions (ADS)
www.adsolutions.org.uk/

Barnardo's, a leading childcare charity with a booklist of useful
publications on 'what works' in key aspects of childcare work
www.barnardos.org.uk

Department for Children, Schools and Families (DCSF)
www.dcsf.gov.uk

Early Years Foundation Stage Framework: a comprehensive
framework combining Birth to Three Matters and Curriculum
Guidance for the FoundationStage and providing standards
for early years development, learning and welfare for children
aged 0 to 5 years
www.birthtofive.org.uk/earlyyearsfoundationstage/eyfs-
framework.aspx

Family Action, formerly Family Welfare Association, supports
families, practically, financially and emotionally
www.familyaction.org.uk

Information on therapeutic approaches to work with families
www.instituteoffamilytherapy.org.uk

Toolkit for commissioners, provided by Parenting UK
www.toolkit.parentinguk.org

6

social work with adults and health-related services

Introduction

Social work with adults involves working with a range of adults entitled to health, social care or social work services by virtue of their vulnerability, frailty or related problems, whether these arise through individual causes, for example diseases such as Alzheimer's, or physical or mental impairments, or through social causes such as discrimination or social exclusion. Hence, social workers carry out a significant proportion of their work in collaboration with health service professionals. This chapter provides a general overview of social work with adults – often disabled, mentally ill or older – who have particular health needs as well as social needs. The field of health and social care, or health and social services, as this area tends to be called, covers a wide span of services and is changing rapidly. It is clear at this early stage in the implementation of the government's personalisation policies that they are likely to have major effects on the practice of social workers, both with people who receive services and with their carers.

Contexts for practice

There are currently almost 80,000 qualified social workers and almost 16,000 students on the GSCC in England and its equivalent bodies in the rest of the UK. This is a small but significant proportion of the total health and social services workforce in the UK, which is about two million. More than one million people work in social care in England, two thirds of these in the private, voluntary and independent sector. The boundaries of these divisions are blurring as new forms of provision, such as integrated services in mental health and disability, take shape.

Adult social care has emerged in the early 21st century in the UK as a distinct branch of the social services, delivered separately from children's services. A number of key strands of ongoing policy and practice development have emerged:

1. Since the 1990s, adult social care has moved into close, more formal partnership arrangements with health services and with other local authority services such as housing. Over the decades since the 1970s, successive UK governments have made efforts to encourage more collaborative working, with the goal of providing people with a 'seamless' service. A system of single assessment was introduced in the 1990s, with the aim of eliminating duplication by different professionals. One aspiration is to move towards the delivery of integrated health and social care services to service users and informal carers.

2. The principle of service user and carer involvement has become established. There is a growing tendency in many western countries towards the growth of consumer movements, parallelling the increasing questioning of the authority of professionals delivering public services. In the 21st century, UK health and welfare policy has emphasised enhancing the participation of people in providing as well as delivering the services they receive. An independent public body, the Commission for Patient and Public Involvement in Health (CPPIH), was set up in 2003 for the purpose of improving the voice of the public in local health services. This led to the establishment of more than 400 patient and public involvement forums. This system was replaced in 2007 by local involvement networks (LINks), extended under the 2007 Local Government and Public Involvement Health Act to include the social care sector. The public members of LINks have legal powers to request information about services from those who commission them and to visit specific services and view them.

3. Since the mid-1990s, the rights of carers to have their needs recognised and met have been reflected in legislation such as the 1995 Carers (Recognition and Services) Act, 2000 Carers and Disabled Children Act and 2004 Carers (Equal Opportunities) Act.

4. Services have become more personalised. Since the 1990s, adults receiving social care services have been able to opt to receive direct payments, to enable them to deploy the resources so as to meet their

own needs. In the early 21st century (DH, 2005a), personalisation has gone further, with the introduction of individual budgets, that service users control themselves.

5. The 2000 Care Standards Act established mechanisms, achieved in England by creating the National Care Standards Commission with equivalent bodies being created in Scotland (Scottish Commission for the Regulation of Care, SCRC), Wales and Northern Ireland, for the regulation of private and voluntary healthcare in England and the regulation and inspection of social care and healthcare services in Wales. It set up new independent councils for the registration of social care workers and developed standards for education and training of social workers in England and Wales and for social work practice. National minimum standards in areas such as domiciliary care (care at home), care homes for adults aged 18 to 65, care homes for older people aged 65+, adult placement schemes and nurses' agencies have been published. The CQC, set up under the 2008 Health and Social Care Act, oversees the regulation and inspection of services.

6. The rights of people to complain about services and 'whistleblow', that is, report shortcomings in a service to a third party or outsider, have been strengthened in the early 21st century.

7. One of the main issues since the 1990s has been the debate about who should pay for which care services for adults. In Scotland, social care services are provided free, whereas in England and Wales they are means-tested. In 2009, the government launched a consultation Green Paper (HM Government, 2009) to gauge public and professional responses to different funding options. Among the options are combinations of free social care for people whose needs are greatest plus means-tested or insurance-based services for other categories of need, with people, by one route or another, contributing to the costs of care.

Inequalities in health, sickness and dying

The wider context of health and social services provision is that since the early 1980s there has been clear evidence from a great mass of undisputed research evidence, brought together in key reports, by Black (1980) and Acheson (1998), that social inequalities (such as child and family poverty, poor housing, poor education and lower-paid employment or unemployment) over at least the last quarter of the 20th century, and probably before that, have persistently led to inequalities in health provision and the outcomes of services, that is, they lead to poorer, more disadvantaged and vulnerable people being more prone to illness and death than better-off people. Many reorganisations of the NHS have been attempts to tackle these and related problems.

Significant government resources are allocated to dealing with the health concerns of adults. Increasingly, government policy emphasises the prevention of illness and health education, development and promotion, but for many adults and older people this is too late. The conditions that adversely affect their health have developed over decades and many older people are unable or unwilling to change their lifestyle sufficiently to make a radical difference to their health.

The experience of chronic illness or a debilitating, possibly terminal, condition is unequally distributed through society and every year, as the population ages, an increasing proportion require social work support. About half a million people die in England each year and most of these – nearly two thirds – are over 75 years old. Most of those who die have been ill with a chronic disease or condition, such as stroke, heart disease, dementia, neurological disease or cancer.

Modernising: from a national illness service to health promotion and development

Strategies to provide health and social care services for people (the publication, *Putting people first: A shared vision and commitment to the transformation of adult social care*, HM Government, 2007) were linked by the government to the wider agenda of change in the health services (the White Paper, *Our health, our care, our say: A new direction for community services*, DH, 2006). (A **White Paper** is a statement of government intentions regarding a new policy.)

At the end of the first decade of the 21st century, financial constraints on the provision of primary health services are leading to the notion of health budgets being geared more to health promotion and the prevention of illness. One radical idea, for instance, is that money should be diverted from health budgets to improve the housing and social environment and reduce people's proneness to accidents, thereby reducing the need for resources in Accident and Emergency (A&E) departments in hospitals.

Preventive health services and health promotion

Partly as a result of the growing recognition of the cost of healthcare and the expanding body of research evidence on the harmful effects of a poor diet and inactive lifestyle, and partly in response to the ageing population, the NHS moved towards a 'preventive' philosophy of health education and promotion during the 1990s and this trend has gathered momentum in the early 21st century.

Both the NHS (under the 1977 NHS Act) and social services (under the 1990 NHS and Community Care Act) have responsibilities for supporting and treating people who have health and care needs. The actual lines of responsibility held by health and social services organisations, and consequently by social workers, are different in the different countries of the UK and, in each locality, operate differently in detail. The main differences are over who pays for particular health and adult social care services. Across the UK, most healthcare is provided free at the point of delivery of services. In Scotland, this also applies to social care for adults, and older people in particular. In England and Wales, local authorities sometimes charge people for specific social care services, but the general rule is that if this involves an element of nursing services then social services should not be involved and the health services should take responsibility for providing it free of charge.

Modernising services

The incoming Labour government's strategy of modernising public services had consequences for the health and social services, as they advanced to the foreground of social policy the notion of citizen choice of services and control over budgets (DH, 1998, 2006; HM Government, 2007). During the early 21st century, the voices of people receiving services have been heard more clearly, demanding more control over their lives. Although disabled people have been at the forefront of these campaigns, older people have contributed vociferously, and because they represent a growing proportion of active voters, politicians and policy makers ignore their views at their own peril. Government policy has shifted from the traditional role of the professionals, including social workers, as making the key decisions on how resources are allocated, to these decisions being made by people who receive services themselves, often with their carers.

A major reform of adult care and related health services took place from the early 1990s. During the 1990s, the implementation of the 1990 NHS and Community Care Act passed by the Conservative government led to the creation of a form of market economy, supported by a system of contracting, with about 80% of community care services being contracted out of local authorities to private and voluntary sector providers. The incoming Labour government of 1997 onwards reinforced the trend of this legislation towards a proliferation of providers of services in a market where the role of health and local authorities shifted towards contracting and commissioning services rather than simply providing them. This has entailed staff learning a new language corresponding to service provision in a market where potential providers compete (see Table 6.1). The continued reform of public services (DH, 1998) included setting standards, introducing tighter mechanisms for monitoring and inspecting performance and developing more joined-up services.

Social work services are provided through systems that assess people's eligibility for services across the health and social care sector. Frameworks are in place that enable a practitioner to reach a preliminary decision about whether a person is likely to meet the criteria making them eligible for services. In general, services provided in this way by the NHS are free, while those provided by social services or adult social care services are means tested, although this is not a universal rule.

Since the mid-1990s people assessed as eligible for services have been able to choose to receive them in the form of direct payments. **Direct payments**, under the 1996 Community Care (Direct Payments) Act, are cash payments that are normally means tested, made to people assessed

Table 6.1: Concepts and components in the process of contracting services

Procurement	The process of contracting, from initially specifying the service, through the process of tendering, to delivery of the contract
Procurement strategy	The workplan for the contracting, which defines the services and assesses what will need to be spent in order to obtain services offering best value and improved quality
Commissioning	The activities associated with following through the process of setting up a new contract
Tendering	The stage of procurement where potential contractors are invited to bid to supply specific services
Contracting	Negotiating a service-level agreement, or written contract, which sets measurable objectives and specifies how the payment regulates and ensures the delivery of specific services at an agreed standard
Service specification	Part of the contract that specifies the minimum level of service required
Service agreement	Part of the contract that specifies what will be delivered and how it will be delivered
Conditions	Part of the contract that normally specifies conditions under which the contract operates

as needing services, who can use them to pay for their own support, in the form of carers (often known as personal assistants) or other provision.

At the heart of the personalisation agenda is the intention to make the views, wishes and choices of the individual recipient of services the first point of reference, when assessing needs and planning services. The aim (Carr, 2008, p 4) is to:

■ work collaboratively with people needing services
■ shape these services to their individual needs
■ ensure that where possible people's difficulties and vulnerabilities are anticipated and prevented, as well as identified and intervened in, helpfully
■ identify the existing strengths in people's lives, such as their carers

■ recognise and give support to their carers
■ develop a responsive system of resources and services which is available to all.

One of the most significant shifts of the implementation of this personalisation agenda is likely to be that social workers move from acting mainly as gatekeepers of resources, to becoming more involved with people who receive services, in terms of enabling them to manage the process of self-assessment where this is appropriate and devising and implementing their own personalised plan, through an individual budget. An **individual budget** is an overall budget allocated by local authority housing, independent living, adult social care, or (in the future) healthcare services, separately or together, through which an individual, a social worker as care manager, a trust, or an indirect provider (these include organisations set up to handle the administration of the individual budgets for service users) can opt to receive a mixture of services and/or cash and can buy services from private, voluntary or community groups or organisations, family or friends, to meet personal needs.

We can see in the following example how an English local authority manages, organises and delivers adult care services.

Pen picture

Haverton Local Authority is applying market principles to the benefit of people who use adult care services and their carers. There are Supporting People teams – multiprofessional teams of health practitioners, social workers and social care workers – which take service users' views and information from relatives into account when deciding on the degree of risk and potential harm to people, the nature of their needs and the level of personal services and family support which is appropriate. Social workers provide professional leadership with these services and specialist help with advice and support with particularly complex cases. Selena is a social worker who acts as the facilitator for the local provider forum. This meets every two months and represents the local organisations and agencies who provide 80% of adult care services to Haverton, through the independent (private and voluntary) sector. Selena works closely with the local commissioning teams employed in the Commissioning Unit that spans health and social services in Haverton, to contract and commission these services. They also work closely with colleagues in the teams of social workers in the safeguarding and residential review teams, who are coordinated by the adult safeguarding coordinator. A panel of service users meets regularly and is consulted throughout the tendering process before commissioning decisions are made. Independent brokers are employed by the Commissioning Unit's teams to help find suitable providers, while once they are identified the care managers in the Supporting People team work closely with the service user and carer/s to carry out the detailed care planning (see Figure 6.1). After the service has been running for some time, Haverton Local Authority is required to carry out a best value review by consulting service users about the service they have received (following the example set out by Evans and Carmichael, 2002). In this case, local authority staff work with the service users in an innovative way to design and carry out most of the review themselves. They reach conclusions about the evaluation of the service and the review process.

Personalised services: stages of work with people

The implementation of the government strategy of personalising people's services has major implications for people. It affects every stage of the delivery of health and social care services (see Table 6.2).

Implementing the personalisation agenda

It is possible that if personalisation was implemented, the stages of practice could be modified so that the assessment stage could be divided into preliminary assessment – where eligibility would be determined – and comprehensive assessment – which would probably be based around the

Figure 6.1: Commissioning and coordinating adult social care services

Table 6.2: Personalisation and delivery of health and social care services	
Stages	**What each stage entails**
Assessment of needs	The social worker and other practitioners work with the service user to compile a unified and comprehensive picture of needs
	Where appropriate, an assessment of the needs of the carer or carers is also carried out, perhaps by a practitioner not compiling the service user's assessment
Planning	The social worker and other practitioners work out with service user and carer/s a detailed plan specifying a schedule for how the needs are going to be met
	The plan includes details on how the individual budget will be used
Implementation	The plan is implemented and its implementation is monitored by the social worker and other practitioners to ensure that this is appropriate
Review/evaluation	At regular intervals, the implementation of the plan is reviewed and at key points it is evaluated

service user's self-assessment. This would be followed by a care planning stage and then service arrangement where the services would be put in place. Subsequently, the service arrangement would be reviewed and evaluated.

Policy priorities regarding health and social care for adults reflect the tension between the aspiration towards joined-up services and the reality that the NHS and social care workforces have distinctively different cultures and significant divergences throughout the four countries of the UK, in the ways health and adult social care services are costed and delivered. In Scotland, for instance, health and social care for adults are provided free of charge at the point of delivery, whereas in England and Wales, health services (with the exception of dental and optical services) are free for adults, but adult social care is normally chargeable, subject to a means test.

Assessment processes

This is a good place, perhaps, to make a general note about the assessment process that will be picked up in subsequent chapters. There have been attempts to simplify assessment thereby removing duplication by different health, social care and allied professionals. A single assessment process has been achieved within adult social care with a care programme approach for people with mental health needs, although there are proposals to develop a common assessment framework across the entire field (DH, 2009b).

Legal basis for practice

Only a selection of relevant legislation that provides the basis for social work practice can be illustrated here. General rights apply to all client groups referred to in Chapters Three to Seven inclusive (see Table 6.3), and legally constituted rights to services (see Table 6.4), which clearly present social work practitioners with the necessity to become familiar with the workings of a significant quantity of legislation.

Table 6.3: Illustrations of legal provisions relating to the rights of adults

1975 Sex Discrimination Act	Duty of public authorities to eliminate illegal sex discrimination
1998 Human Rights Act[a]	Upholds a range of basic human rights
2006 Equality Act	(Updated the 1975 Sex Discrimination Act.) Duty of public authorities to promote equality of treatment of people

Note: [a] This ties in with the UNCHR and the ECHR (see Chapter Three).

Table 6.4: Illustrations of legal provisions regarding rights to services

1970 Local Authority Social Services Act
1983 Mental Health Act
1989 Children Act
1990 NHS and Community Care Act
1995 Carers (Recognition and Services) Act
2000 Care Standards Act
2000 Carers and Disabled Children Act
2003 Mental Health (Care and Treatment) Scotland Act
2004 Carers (Equal Opportunities) Act
2004 Children Act
2005 Mental Capacity Act
2007 Protection of Vulnerable Adults (Scotland) Act
2007 Mental Health Act

Working with carers

More than five million people in the UK carry out informal (that is, unpaid) caring for relatives and close friends, making an estimated contribution to the economy equivalent to a remarkable £87 billion, exceeding the £82 billion total spending on health services in the UK in 2006-07 and exceeding by more than fourfold the £19.3 billion spent by local authorities on social care services for adults and children (Buckner and Yeandle, 2007).

These informal carers may be caring for one or more relatives, are usually unpaid and are often attempting to balance the competing demands of the household, employment and doing the caring. When a person is being assessed for community care, the professional will ask them whether they consider they have one or more carers and, where appropriate, will contact these carers. An informal carer has rights, as an outcome of progress with carers' policy and practice made since the early 1990s. This has culminated in a carers' strategy (DH, 2008b) which:

- recognises that carers' circumstances have not been met and their needs recognised previously;
- proposes short-term measures to alleviate some of the most major concerns of carers;
- sets out a longer-term strategy to support carers.

Carers are already entitled, under the 1995 Carers (Recognition and Services) Act, the 2000 Carers and Disabled Children Act and the 2004 Carers (Equal Opportunities) Act, to assessment of their needs and to their educational and leisure needs being met. For instance, they can arrange with social work and social care staff, respite services for the person they care for, so that they can continue to 'have a life' apart from their caring.

Support to informal carers – who comprise both children and adults – is often invisible, and carers often suffer through themselves having inadequate support. Campaigns by carers through their organisations have contributed to government policy initiatives to support carers and raise their take-up of benefits to which they are legally entitled (DH, 2008b).

Young carers

A significant proportion of carers are young carers. Estimates vary, but about 175,000 children and young people caring for people – children and adults – were identified in the UK Census of 2001, and an official estimate two years later was that there could be 150,000 (DfES, 2003, p 43). An accurate total of young carers is not possible, since for different reasons many are unlikely to declare to outsiders their role in the family. They may be embarrassed, or they may fear the family being split up if the person cared for is revealed to the authorities as unable to cope.

Several national organisations and many local groups such as Carers UK (www.carersuk.org) and the Princess Royal Trust for Carers (www.carers. org) have developed to give carers support. Many people do not realise that under current legislation as carers they have legal rights to assessment, their own planning and resources. This lack of awareness extends to carers' lack of knowledge of their entitlement to carers' allowances and benefits.

National end-of-life care strategy

The government's end-of-life care strategy (DH, 2008a) involves the development of an integrated approach by PCTs and local authorities to commissioning and developing care for individuals at the end of life. More than half (58%) of deaths take place in NHS hospitals and about 18% occur at home, 17% in care homes, 4% in hospices and 3% in other locations. Central to the end-of-life strategy is the aim that dying people should be treated with respect and be able to die with dignity as and where they wish, in familiar or sympathetic surroundings, in the presence of family and/or friends and without unnecessary pain or discomfort.

Social workers may manage the care of dying people in different settings, in:

- people's own homes
- hospitals
- care homes
- hospices, developed in the voluntary sector since the first hospice was created by Dame Cicely Saunders at St Christopher's Hospice in 1967.

Community care

The 1990 NHS and Community Care Act 1990 marked three significant shifts in policy and practice, even though this legislation was not the first sign of progress in any of these areas:

- It advanced the cause of services for people in the community and, where possible, their delivery at home, rather than through residential provision.
- It promoted service provision by private and voluntary agencies.
- It pushed closer together the healthcare organisations and professionals and those in social services, in the provision of health and social care services.

Social services (including adult social care) departments are responsible for assessing a person's needs for community care services under the 1990 NHS and Community Care Act. They do this jointly with the health services where the person also has health needs. This assessment grades the needs of the person in four bands: critical, substantial, moderate or low (see Table 6.5). This assessment takes into account the wishes and independence of the person, their health and safety, their family life including any potential or existing support available from carers, their capacity to cope with everyday life and to engage with the community. The local authority sets the eligibility criteria for services using a fair access to care services framework (DH, 2003) as a standard, and decides at what level the service must be provided, usually when the level of need is either substantial or critical. Eligibility for continuing care – in general, the responsibility of the NHS – is based on a person's assessed health needs and not on a particular diagnosis or condition, their financial means or on available resources. By agreeing a national framework for eligibility for services and funding in England and Wales, the government aims to ensure decisions are made consistently throughout different regions and localities, thereby avoiding what has been referred to as health services available only as a 'postcode lottery' (that is, varying according to where you live).

Table 6.5: The four bands of needs	
Low	Inability to carry out one or more day-to-day routines, in looking after oneself or managing the home
	Lack of engagement in one or two aspects of education, learning or work
	Lack of one or two support systems and relationships
	Not undertaking one or two family and other social roles
Moderate	Inability to carry out several day-to-day routines, in looking after oneself or managing the home
	Lack of engagement in several aspects of education, learning or work
	Lack of several support systems and relationships
	Not undertaking several family and other social roles
Substantial	Only partial choice or control over immediate setting
	Previous abuse or neglect
	Inability to carry out the majority of day-to-day routines, in looking after oneself or managing the home
	Lack of engagement in many aspects of education, learning or work
	Lack of most support systems and relationships
	Not undertaking most family and other social roles
Critical	Life-threatening current circumstances
	Little or no choice or control over immediate setting
	Significant health problems now or in immediate future
	An inability to carry out one or more day-to-day routines, in looking after oneself or managing the home
	Lack of engagement in one or two aspects of education, learning or work
	Lack of one or two support systems and relationships
	Not undertaking essential family and other social roles

Settings for practice

The settings for social work with adults vary widely and may include the following:

- hospital-based social work
- work by specialist social work teams working with children, families and adults
- work by specialist liaison older people's mental health teams
- work with people through home care
- day services
- work with people in residential settings
- work with people in nursing homes
- hospice-based work and associated home care
- specialist social work with different types of later life problems and issues
- intermediate care
- considering the need of people for housing support and for housing-related services including tele-care.

These are only illustrative and the variety of settings listed here could be much longer.

Hospital-based social work

The main purposes of hospital-based social work are to help people with the personal and social aspects of their condition. Admission and discharge are particularly traumatic for many people, as well as for their carers, but problems and issues can arise at any time during a person's stay in hospital. Social workers are called on by healthcare professionals when the nature of other personal, family and social problem's impacts adversely on a person's recovery from an illness, condition, surgery or other treatment.

End-of-life care is the term used to apply to measures to meet the needs of people who are dying, across the population as a whole, while **palliative care** is the term used to refer to specialist health and social services for people near the end of their lives. Despite the assumption we might make that government policy directed towards establishing a society-wide strategy for end-of-life services applies to older people (DH, 2008a), some of the more demanding social work practice is with other age groups. It is important to appreciate that work with dying people has relevance throughout the life course. Kübler-Ross (1982) gives detailed case studies of working with people who are dying. She shows how working with a therapist can help other professionals to understand what the person is going through, equipping them better to cope with the person's needs. For instance, interpreting a child's paintings helped to assess the extent to which the child's spirit was in harmony with the deterioration of her body (Kübler-Ross, 1982, pp 65-9).

Some people die in their own way, without the presence of a hospice. For others, the support of a hospice enables them to die in the way they choose, perhaps spending some time in the hospice and eventually dying at home. Social workers working with health professionals in hospices are able to help people to die with dignity and their families to cope with bereavement.

Approaches to practice

Social work with adults draws on many social work approaches and methods. Safeguarding work is increasingly important, but the priority given to this should not detract the attention of professionals from the need to acquire and maintain other areas of expertise, in therapeutic work, for instance. Examples of different approaches are given in subsequent chapters.

Mental capacity or mental disorder

People's interests may need protecting if and when, for reasons of ill health or a deteriorating mental condition, they become unable to make decisions. Their rights are protected under the 2005 Mental Capacity Act. Social workers and other professionals such as solicitors are responsible for taking professional action in such circumstances. Solicitors help with framing legal documents, including wills, so as to apply **lasting power**

of attorney, which in effect is the advance decision a person makes to appoint another person to act on their behalf, should they become incapable of doing so for themselves. Social workers play a key role in contributing to the assessment of the person in such circumstances and ensuring that subsequent decisions must be made in the best interests of that person.

Social workers often work with people who have problems of mental health, mental instability or mental disturbance. In general terms, issues of mental illness and disorder are dealt with under the 1983 and 2007 Mental Health Acts; issues associated with a person not being able to manage their personal affairs are dealt with under the 2005 Mental Capacity Act.

Practice

Personalisation in practice

Personalisation is built around individualised budgets for people who use services and expresses the principles of empowering service users, increasing their participation and maximising their choice over the nature of services delivered to meet their needs.

The strengths perspective, developed by Dennis Saleeby (2002), involves assessing people's needs from their strengths and potential rather than simply their deficits, building on their existing knowledge, skills and resources to enable them to cope with challenges and difficulties. Person-centred assessment involves keeping individual needs at the centre throughout the process of assessment and ensuring that the person's perception of his or her basic needs is always taken into consideration at every stage. In these terms, analysis of basic needs is more holistic, assessing the needs of the whole person: the stage of the life course reached, the capacity of relatives, partners and carers to respond to needs and the resources available in the family, neighbourhood and wider environment.

The following example shows how the principles of personalisation contribute to a person's quality of life in practice.

Example

Donna was diagnosed with osteoporosis 10 years ago when she was 55. She had an individualised budget at that stage and after making lifestyle changes she reduced this, as she felt she no longer needed the full range of support services. She has now been diagnosed with a mild condition that affects her physical mobility, but does not affect her lifestyle, provided she can be supplied with additional health and social care services. She recently asked her social worker, a member of the In Control panel who works in the multiprofessional team supporting her, for her individualised budget to be increased and this request was approved immediately.

Donna uses her budget to buy herself three personal assistants, who work on a rota, to enable her to maintain her voluntary work from Monday to Friday. Her daughter stays with her at weekends and takes care of her needs. Donna also uses her budget to buy certain items of equipment to help her maintain her busy lifestyle.

With the help of this individualised budget and personalised services, Donna is able to maintain her independent lifestyle at present.

Drug and alcohol problems

Often, adults, especially parents, with mental health problems, who also misuse drugs and alcohol, have seriously affected relationships with others. The combined effects of such problems impair their capacity to parent and make their children vulnerable to abuse and neglect, as well as affecting their interaction with other relatives and the local community. According to Cleaver et al (2007), children are more likely to be damaged by their parents' misuse of alcohol and drugs than if there is domestic violence.

Implications of personalisation for practice

People's individual budgets span the health and social care services, so the implications of personalising services through them are very major, for agencies, professional social workers, other practitioners and staff and, last but by no means least, for people receiving services and their carers. On the negative side, the provision of integrated services may be inhibited by technical, legal and accountability barriers to money being supplied from both health and social services or social care services as a single funding stream. On the positive side, the implementation of personalisation through such means as direct payments (see DH, 2004b) offers service users increased choice and can ensure that professionals have enhanced autonomy to manage and deliver effective services. However, it also presents increased risks in circumstances where service users have the opportunity to make their own decisions in favour of a freer lifestyle, which heightens health and safety hazards and risks to them. The consequences of personalisation for social workers and other practitioners is that they probably have to spend more time than hitherto with services users and carers who have individual budgets, carrying out the service users' assessments, assessing the needs of carers, planning how they are going to use their individual budgets and helping them to gain the necessary knowledge and skills they may need to manage their budgets.

Pen picture

Helga is 72. She has asked for personalised services, which entails her having direct payments. However, she has severe physical impairments and is determined to continue her active lifestyle. Her social worker has been asked by the In Control panel of the local authority to carry out a comprehensive risk assessment for her before she goes on to direct payments.

Helga's social worker decides that the best way forward is for Helga to receive advice from Helping You Directly, a local voluntary organisation which, for a fee, provides legal and administrative support for people receiving direct payments, to enable them to manage them independently. The social worker also arranges for Helga's direct payments to be monitored regularly to make sure that she is managing them and is receiving good quality support services.

Helga's social worker regards the success of Helga's personalised services as due to the flexibility and autonomy of professional decisions she is able to make, in consultation with Helga. They are both empowered and more independent through this approach to personalisation.

One implication of this work is that Helga's social worker is playing a very active part in advocacy work with Helga and is supporting her in several ways in achieving independence through managing her own individual budget as part of her personalised services.

SUMMARY

This chapter has shown that the implementation of the government's personalisation agenda has major implications for local health and social care services and is playing a major part in transforming these services. Social workers' responsibilities are affected by these changes and new opportunities for practice are being created, often working with other agencies and professions.

RECOMMENDED READING

An excellent up-to-date discussion of social care ideas and practice: Payne, M. (2008) *Social care practice in context*, Basingstoke: Palgrave.

A good introduction to the field of health and social care: Glasby, J. (2007) *Understanding health and social care*, Bristol: The Policy Press.

Useful discussion of issues and practices in joint working in health and social care: Glasby, J. and Dickinson, H. (2008) *Partnership working in health and social care*, Bristol: The Policy Press.

WEB LINKS

Framework for safeguarding adults
www.adss.org.uk/publications/guidance/safeguarding.pdf

Information on the latest policy changes in adult social care
www.dh.gov.uk/en/SocialCare/Socialcarerefrom/index/htm

Up-to-date information on personalisation from the Care Services Improvement Partnership
www.networks.csip.org.uk/personalisation/index.
cfm?pid=782

7

social work with older people

Introduction

Social workers are engaged in work with increasing numbers of older people in society. Many older people suffer from the consequences of living longer in old age – an increasing complexity of personal and social problems due to infirmity, including loss of mental as well as physical faculties, which contribute to a lack of mobility and isolation. Let us be clear, however; ageing is not always associated with physical and mental deterioration. Analysis of data from the General Household Survey for 2001 (Walker et al, 2002) indicates that not more than 3% of older people ever rely on social services. Most people live independently into old age and die without a prolonged period of infirmity or dependence on others.

Social workers play an important role in advancing practice with older people, particularly people whose problems put them at greater risk of neglect or harm. Social work with older people is a growing specialism, despite the fact that adult social care services cater for the basic social care needs of older people. Social workers become involved with older people whose personal and social needs are more complex and require a greater degree of skilled work. This occurs, for instance, where people need professional social work support in brokering their personalised services. It also occurs where the complexity and extent of people's problems calls on a higher level of professional expertise, as in work with people near the end of their lives (known as 'end-of-life care'). Professional work with people who are dying is known as palliative care. Of course, even though the majority of end-of-life or palliative care is with older people, children and adults may reach the end of their life at any age. The fact that this is not expected makes it likely that some

149

individuals and families may not cope, and consequently it is important for social workers to be equipped with the qualities and skills to work with them. Some practitioners may take on this work full time, permanently, while others will undertake it for a limited period.

Contexts for practice

We live in an ageing society, because people are living longer. The age at which people are regarded as old is shifting, as life expectancies extend. In the 19th century, the average life expectancy in Britain was in the early forties – just over halfway through the average life expectancy of the early 21st century. The UK, in common with many other western countries, has a disproportionately old age profile, that is, a large segment of the population are growing older, while the number of younger people, relatively speaking, is declining. In 2007 the proportion of under-16s in the population (less than 20%) was less than the proportion of pensioners. People over 80 (4.5%, over 2,700,000) constituted the fastest growing group in the population (see www.statistics.gov.uk/focuson/olderpeople/).

These changes are taking place partly because of improved lifestyles, diets and the successes of health and social services over the past century and a half. People are living longer and advances in medical research, understanding of illnesses and conditions, as well as the growing range of effective treatments, means that people are kept active and reasonably healthy, further into old age than ever before. As people gradually age, however, their ailments and conditions increase. For some, growing older is a process of gradual decline, unfortunately leading to an extended period of dependence on other people that creates an ever-increasing burden for the health and social services.

Privilege extends into old age. Social inequalities of income, wealth, housing and education affect people's health, proneness to illness and premature death. In other words, the health and well-being of older people reflects similar inequalities to the rest of the life course. Poorer people in less advantaged social and occupational groups tend to be more sick and die younger than better-off people. People in different ethnic communities – not the dominant one in their locality – tend to be more likely to be excluded from access to services for older people. Geographical inequalities persist, amplified where people cannot drive or do not have access to public transport, for whatever reason – disability, frailness or non-availability of buses or trains. For these, and other related reasons, older people living in rural settings tend to experience more difficulty gaining access to services than those in urban settings.

Among the older groups in the population, women increasingly predominate, in a pattern often referred to as the feminisation of ageing. This tends to mean that older, dependent and vulnerable women – whether at home being cared for by a sister or other informal carer or in a residential home being cared for by an employed care assistant – tend to be looked after by women. This is not exclusively the case, however, and increasing numbers of older men living longer either live alone or are in a caring, or cared for, relationship with an older woman.

We have seen above that a growing proportion of the population of western countries is what we term 'older'. Nowadays, terms such as 'old' and 'the elderly' are less preferred, as the former reinforces a label that could be used in an ageist and discriminatory way and the latter refers to, or defines, the whole person entirely in terms of their age.

The UK follows the trend of other western countries, towards an increasing proportion of older people in the population (expected to treble over the next 30 years), as the health and living standards of people improve and they tend to survive later into old age. More than 20 million people in the UK – a third of the population – are over 50 and over one million are 85 or over. Nearly 20% of the population – over 11 million – are over retirement age. The average life span of a person in mid-Victorian Britain was in the early forties, whereas nowadays it is the late seventies, with women surviving slightly longer than men. The average life expectancies of women and men at birth are 81.1 and 76.9 years respectively. At 65, women and men can expect to live till 84.6 and 81.9 respectively. This increase is because by that age, people who were less healthy and had a significantly lower life expectancy have already died. There are three times as many women over 90 as men.

The inevitable consequence of this is that people are 'older' for a greater proportion of their lives than formerly. However, there is resistance by professionals and among 'older' activists to using the term 'old' on the grounds that this is a rather bleak and irreversible label. This links with a wider argument that many social, policy and professional attitudes towards older people are somewhat ageist.

All of the above features of growing older in modern society affect social relationships, between family members, between spouses and between carer and cared-for people. Research indicates that gender is an important variable, in that women under 65 tend to take on caring roles more than men under 65. Other family members, too, play important roles as carers. Often caring responsibilities skip a generation – grandparents are available to look after grandchildren while parents are at work and, in reverse, daughters and sons may offer accommodation in their home and some home care not only for parents but also sometimes for grandparents as well.

Implications for social workers

Social work is required when people become physically and mentally vulnerable through frailty, disability or cognitive impairment (Phillips et al, 2006, p 36). Social work takes place against this backcloth and social workers who work with older people need to be sensitive to their feelings about increasing vulnerability, while recognising their wish not to be forgotten, dismissed as a useless burden or discriminated against. Ideally, social work sets out to provide a positive framework of principles and practice, which gives older people the support and services they require in order to maximise the quality of their remaining life span.

Legal basis for practice

Because growing older is accompanied by a growing number of related but distinct problems of mental and physical impairment, as people's bodies and minds age, legal measures aiming to protect the interests and rights of older people tend to come in the guise of many different pieces of legislation. Unfortunately, the double bind for older people is that they have a right to be treated equally with other people and it is not pleasant to have to use their age as the means to achieve this equality of services. From a critical point of view, we can argue that while principles of anti-ageism make it desirable not to treat older people primarily on the basis of their entitlement through reaching a particular age, the lack of location in one legal enactment of all services for older people does not make it easy for older people to assert their rights to appropriate services.

The roots of social care and social work services for older people lie in the 1948 National Assistance Act, the 1970 Local Authority Social Services Act which established overarching social services and many subsequent Acts updating and consolidating this and other related legislation, such as the 2006 NHS Act (Table 7.1).

Table 7.1: Relevant legal provisions

Act or report	Main provisions
1948 National Assistance Act	Community and residential provision for older and disabled people
1986 Health Services and Public Health Act	Welfare of older people, duty to provide for
2005 Mental Capacity Act	Provides advocacy and enduring power of attorney for vulnerable (including older) people
1990 NHS and Community Care Act	The most significant legislation of the past two decades, encouraging community care, with the aim of producing more economic services
2006 NHS Act	Provides aftercare after discharge from hospital, domiciliary care

National standards for services for older people

The government has published standards of services that it expects local providers of services for older people to meet (DH, 2001b). Among the most important of these standards are the following:

1. Eliminating discrimination on the grounds of age
2. Promoting person-centred care
3. Developing integrated services, particularly between health and social care and social work
4. Establishing intermediate care at home or in care settings (intermediate care is care between hospital and more independent living at home)
5. Enhancing hospital services
6. Developing services for preventing strokes
7. Promoting the principle of people living a healthy and active life
8. Reducing accidents to older people, such as falls

This set of standards complements the general charter for long-term care (DH and DETR, 1999) outlined in Chapter Six.

Mental capacity

A person's wishes can be overridden where they become mentally disordered, or where they are living in unhygienic circumstances and the social worker, or another social services professional, brings this to the notice of a Magistrates' Court and the magistrate orders them to be moved to Part III accommodation under the 1948 National Assistance Act. The 2005 Mental Capacity Act attempts to anticipate and prevent such problems arising by allowing the person, while still mentally able, to nominate another person to handle their financial and associated affairs and to enable services to be provided in their best interests. Thus, relatives, friends and professionals including the social worker can use the 2005 Mental Capacity Act to deal with issues associated with a person not being able to manage their personal affairs.

Settings for practice

Social work with older people takes place in various settings: sheltered housing, residential homes, nursing homes, day services and centres and **domiciliary care** – known as home care and associated with providing support for people staying in their own homes. While the popular perception may be that people inevitably move into residential settings as they grow older, in reality the majority of people grow older in their own homes. The *National Service Framework for older people* (DH, 2001b) includes the standard encouraging **intermediate care** – intended to be integrated measures to prevent a person being admitted to hospital needing acute treatment.

Most older people live out their lives without ever using day or domiciliary services or staying in a residential or nursing home. However, these facilities form a continuum of support from the least intensive to the most intensive (see Figure 7.1), and are available to support older people who become increasingly infirm and frail with advancing age.

Figure 7.1: Continuum of services for older people

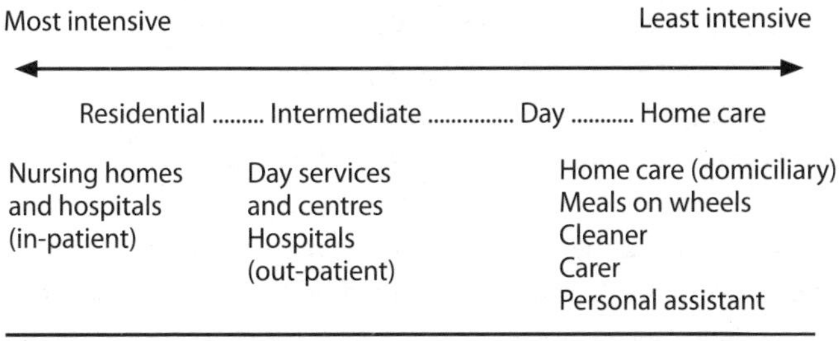

Most intensive   Least intensive

←———————————————————————————————→

Residential .... Intermediate .... Day .... Home care

Nursing homes and hospitals (in-patient)	Day services and centres Hospitals (out-patient)	Home care (domiciliary) Meals on wheels Cleaner Carer Personal assistant

Government policy in the early 21st century is built around the idea of personalising services, or person-centred care, as this is often called in work with older people. There are four main components of this:

■ fitting services to people's needs rather than fitting people to available services
■ enabling people to choose and control the kinds of services they use
■ ensuring that the services maximise their independence
■ providing services that give access to social, community, leisure and educational activities.

The goal is to provide people with services which do not just offer 'comfort and care' (which many people regard as condescending and reflecting 'ageist' assumptions) but also maximise quality of life. Social workers with older people often work 'uphill' as it were, using anti-discriminatory and equality-based strategies to tackle widespread ageist attitudes towards older people, which the *National Service Framework for older people* (DH, 2001b) and *Fair access to care services* (DH, 2003) measures are also intended to combat (Phillips et al, 2006, p 78). **Anti-discriminatory approaches** is the term used for policies and practices that aim to tackle forms of discrimination such as racism, ageism, sexism and disablism. **Ageism** is the term used to refer to unfair or discriminatory attitudes towards, and treatment of, people on the basis of their age.

Approaches to practice

Approaches to providing older people's services draw on different forms of care. Let us clarify the distinctions between social work, social care and personal care, used in these settings.

Social work with older people is a specialised aspect of their general social care, and yet is a more encompassing perspective on 'the personal' (the individual) and 'the social' (the family, group, home, community and societal environments with which the individual interacts), focusing on meeting their more complex needs with a holistic concern for their quality of life, fulfilment, health and well-being – for instance, if they are vulnerable, have been abused, have complex family problems or mental health problems, or need end-of-life care in a hospice or at home. At a more basic level, **social care** includes the wide span of the practical and emotional support services a person needs, ensuring, for instance, they are adequately housed, are warm and are properly fed. **Personal care** means almost the same as social care and covers a wider scope than **personal hygiene**, which, as it sounds, refers to ensuring bodily functions are managed hygienically, including washing and cleanliness.

Dignity in care is an essential component of the quality of care provided for older people and contributes crucially to the way professionals, including social workers, interact with them. Research has produced key indicators for dignity in care for older people (Magee et al, 2008), which comprise four intersecting themes that can be used as a starting point for social workers and other professionals, so that they can generate their own detailed checklist to ensure good practice (see Table 7.2).

Table 7.2: **Checklist of areas forming the basis of dignity in work with older people**	
Choice	This entails making sure that older people have the necessary practical support and the level and detail of information that is sufficient to enable them to make choices which should meet their needs
Control	This entails professionals having due regard for the lifestyle and wishes of older people and enabling them to participate fully in decisions made about the services provided to them
Staff attitudes	This entails professionals always acting with respect for older people, showing courtesy and being appropriately sensitive in all their work with them
Facilities	This refers to the requirement that professionals provide facilities for older people that are appropriate to meet their needs, and are of a high standard, for example, clean and fit for purpose

These principles apply generally to work with older people and to palliative and end-of-life care (see Chapter Four). A similar list of eight pillars of good practice has been developed by the Home Life Project (see www.myhomelife.org.uk/ProjectThemes.htm), an initiative to establish a baseline of good quality in care homes. The following is a slightly edited version of their list of good practice:

1. Managing the process of somebody moving into a care home, including setting up visits first and ensuring that a designated member of staff in the home helps the person through the transition.
2. Ensuring that the person can exercise choices and control over day-to-day aspects of living, such as what to wear.
3. Making sure the residents in the home as a community are able to take part in running aspects of the home.
4. Ensuring that the residents can take part in decisions together and have minimum restrictions consistent with safeguarding them and meeting their welfare needs.

5. Promoting the health of residents and making sure that meal times are pleasurable and that they do not suffer lack of nourishment.
6. Promoting good quality end-of-life care.
7. Making sure that the staff are appropriate and have support in their professional development.
8. Ensuring that the staff develop a positive culture and work effectively as a team.

Practice

Many conditions and problems bring about social work involvement with older people. This section discusses the main features of practice and illustrates work with some major groups of service users. It is important to bear in mind that social work with older people entails developing packages of care to provide them with the support that enables them to continue to live as independently as possible.

Integrated practice

A key component of practice with older people is its basis in integrated provision. This is associated with the principle of partnership working, both with professional colleagues and with service users and carers. The policy goal of delivering seamless services, in effect, means that multiprofessional working overcomes the fragmentation of provision resulting from the involvement of many different health and social professions in meeting the needs of one person.

Single assessment and eligibility for services

A good example of the policy goal of integrated practice is the implementation of models of single assessment – known as single assessment in England (DH, 2001c), Wales and Northern Ireland, and single shared assessment in Scotland (Scottish Executive, 2002). According to Standard 2 in the *National Service Framework for older people* (DH, 2001b), this entails less duplication of effort and is less anxiety provoking for the service user. At the start of the 21st century, the government introduced measures – fair access to care – to improve the consistency of access to services (DH, 2003), that include defining categories of risk – low, moderate, substantial and critical – to determine which cases are entitled to services.

Assessment also includes assessment of the needs of carers, under the 1995 Carers (Recognition and Services) Act. The right of the carer to assessment was extended under the 2000 Carers and Disabled Children Act.

Assessment should be holistic – that is, taking into account all relevant aspects of a person's life, such as physical, emotional, sexual, social, leisure, cultural, religious and spiritual aspects and needs. Assessment should also include assessing the person's vulnerabilities as well as their strengths, resources and areas of expertise. Sometimes there is a tendency to focus on people's disabilities and deterioration, rather than their remaining abilities. However, **risk assessment** is important, as it highlights hazards and dangers and the person's proneness, for instance, to accidents in the kitchen when cooking, through failing eyesight or arthritic hands.

Care planning, intervention and review

Practitioners are responsible for ensuring that service users' and carers' assessed needs are met, through the processes of translating assessments into care plans. **Planning** is the activity of negotiating with service users and carers their expectations, translating these into a practical and detailed programme for specifying objectives and how these should be met. This is, or should be, done in partnership with people who use services and their carers. Care planning can take account of areas of risk, by ensuring the person has a personal assistant when cooking, or has the hot main meal of the day supplied through meals on wheels.

Intervention can take the form of the practitioner using a variety of social work approaches (see Chapter One for details of these, such as networking, task-centred work, crisis intervention, counselling or cognitive behavioural work) in work with service users and carers. **Networking** can be particularly important, identifying potential supportive people during the assessment and incorporating them into the care planning and intervention.

Monitoring includes the monitoring involved in safeguarding people and therefore relates to managing risks, but is also used in a more routine sense to refer to the continuous checking and re-checking of the person's situation, to ensure that the care plan is used as a dynamic and flexible means of meeting their changing needs.

Safeguarding older people

Older people are vulnerable to abuse from many directions – relatives, friends, neighbours and professionals. Abuse may take many forms and their diversity makes it difficult to categorise. The 2006 Safeguarding Vulnerable Groups Act sets out measures to protect **older** people. The government publication *No secrets* (DH and Home Office, 2000) requires improved coordination between agencies. The Protection of Vulnerable Adults scheme was replaced in 2009 by a vetting and barring scheme that lists people not permitted to work with vulnerable adults. Often emotional and financial abuse, for instance, run together. People suffering from the more advanced symptoms of dementia need particular safeguarding against the responses of other people to their condition. There are occasions when people need to be protected so as to stop them either from harming themselves or others. A report by the CSCI (2007) identifies problems in the setting of clear boundaries in what is acceptable, when restraining older people.

Working with older people with eating disorders

It is vital for older people to maintain their diet in order to maximise their quality of life and health and well-being. Conditions such as bulimia and anorexia are eating disorders that affect more than a million people in the UK, whose origins are poorly understood but the consequences of which can be devastating. **Bulimia** is a condition involving binge eating followed by use of laxatives, diuretics, purging and associated self-hating. Whereas **anorexia** is a loss of appetite caused by mouth or throat cancer or similar medical condition, **anorexia nervosa** is a psychological or mental health condition involving a prolonged unwillingness to eat, for complex reasons that appear to be associated with the person's self-perception, which can lead to fatal weight loss. Such disorders are more commonly associated with younger people, but research shows that almost three quarters of deaths from anorexia nervosa in Canada, for instance, are among older people (see www.publicaffairs.ubc.ca/media/releases/1996/mr-96-85.html).

Work with people with eating disorders is demanding, because their origins are complex and it is often easy to mistake the signs of an eating disorder with the general signs of growing old. Social workers may be working with an older person, with a range of other professionals – health visitors, GPs, nurses and occupational therapists – and will encounter a possible eating disorder. It will be necessary to:

- overcome the possibility that their patterns of weight gain and loss are due to other causes
- be sensitive to remarks by the older person about eating problems
- respond to signs of prolonged or repeated patterns of poor appetite
- be aware of missed, skimmed or rejected meals
- prevent the catastrophic consequences for the older person whose bodily reserves are less than those of a younger person.

Working with people with dementia

About 700,000 people in the UK have dementia (a progressive worsening of a person's memory and personality, leading to isolation, deteriorating relationships and eventually complete mental incapacity, double incontinence, physical decline and death). This number is likely to double over the next 30 years. During this period the cost to the UK economy of dealing with dementia of about £17 billion a year is likely to treble to more than £50 billion a year (DH, 2009a, p 9).

Dementia, of which Alzheimer's disease is one specific syndrome, is a progressive, currently incurable, condition which has a tragic effect not only on the individual sufferer but also on relationships with others – relatives and friends – inside and outside the family. Dementia causes a progressive decline in the ability to remember, reason, communicate and to carry out basic personal and social tasks. The symptoms of dementia may include depression, mood changes (people may become volatile), an uncharacteristic lack of normal social inhibitions (people may become outspoken), aggression (normally mild people may become verbally or physically violent), depression or psychosis (a symptom of mental disturbance involving distortion or loss of contact with reality).

Historically, some GPs hesitated to diagnose a person as having dementia, especially in the early stages when the condition was mild, because of the widespread view that the condition was progressive and incurable and there was no advantage in telling people any earlier than was absolutely necessary. Consequently, family members often found out much later and had to cope simultaneously with the shock and with the more serious later symptoms of the condition. The Alzheimer's Society published a report calculating that over the coming 30 years there would be a doubling in the number of people suffering from Alzheimer's disease and a trebling of related costs to £50 billion a year. Partly in response to such predictions, the government has developed a strategy (DH, 2009a) aiming to ensure improvements in services to people with dementia, through:

- early diagnosis
- fuller information to people
- positive intervention
- improved care and support.

The aim is that, through earlier and more proactive services, people are better placed to adjust to the condition, before its consequences become devastating for families.

Pen picture

Thelma is 65 and is in the early stages of Alzheimer's disease. Her husband Frank, 78, has confided in his social worker that he needs a break and she has arranged several short periods of respite care in a residential nursing home. Thelma has begun wandering at night and the care staff in the home have become concerned at her sudden mood changes when they try to prevent her wandering into other people's rooms and attempting to leave the premises. Professionals working with Thelma have advised Frank that he can expect changes of mood and temperament as her condition advances.

Attempts were made to persuade Thelma verbally when she wandered – and to use sedatives at night to help her sleep, with Frank's informed consent, where necessary. **Informed consent** is the term used to refer to situations where all the consequences of agreeing to a course of action are explained to people and care is taken to ensure they understand them, before they are asked formally whether they give consent.

Pen picture

Rosa is 80, frail and suffering from several serious medical conditions that require frequent interventions. She was a senior nurse herself and can be an 'impatient patient'. Her social worker has remained supportive throughout a period when she was financially and emotionally abused by relatives and carers. Her social worker is committed to ensuring that Rosa is treated with dignity and respect, by all who come into contact with her. The social worker undertakes some life history work with Rosa, helping her to fulfil her dream of writing her autobiography. This activity boosts Rosa's self-esteem, contributes to her coping with bouts of severe depression and, as it draws in other professionals to her project, becomes a vital ingredient in her person-centred care.

Working with transitions

Social workers are responsible for ensuring that transitions – such as moving from hospital back home or moving from home into sheltered housing or a residential home – are managed with the service user in a sensitive way. Losing your home through having to move may be particularly traumatic for an older person who has become emotionally attached to their home through the memories it holds. This is particularly important where the person has hearing or sight impairments or cognitive impairments and has no close relatives or friends to advocate for them during the process.

Social workers have a duty to attend carefully to conditions in care homes when visiting older people. It is incumbent on social workers, as on other professionals as well as residents' relatives and friends when they visit, to be alert to the possibility of abuse and to 'whistleblow' where appropriate.

Key issues

In order to work with older people, social workers need to draw on many areas of expertise. It is easy to under-estimate the strength of emotions people undergo as they face growing old and the problems of ageing. Social workers need to be able to manage conflicts that may occur between family members. For instance, it is not uncommon for the carer and the person with dementia to come into conflict over what is best for them. It is not necessarily of benefit to an older person for the carer to be their advocate. It may be preferable to have an outsider to the family appointed as an independent mental capacity advocate under the 2005 Mental Capacity Act.

The social worker may be the independent person who can appreciate the experiences and wishes of the older person and is able to act as the broker and negotiator to ensure that the person receives the services she or he wants.

The social worker can also act as the supporter and adviser to the carer, or several carers. It may be that the complexity and depth of issues in the family require a social worker with the older person and a different social worker with the carer. The social worker needs to consult with the carer and help the carer to develop a self-assessment of needs and to build a plan in the light of this. Resources such as sources of further information about entitlements and access to support networks and

total number of impaired or disabled people in the UK is not
an official estimate is that this is around 10 million – one in
population of about 60 million people (DWP, 2004). Learning
a general term used, often unhelpfully when perceived as a
label, to refer to people who have difficulties with learning
profound learning difficulties affect a relatively small, but still
significant, proportion of disabled people in general – about
survey found that there is widespread ignorance about
ng disability is, three quarters of people not being able to
he (Scopulus, 2008).

d disability are among the more challenging areas in which
kes place. There are two main reasons for this:

d disabled people have increasingly criticised dominant
professional attitudes to their impairments.
d disabled people have advocated policies and practices
ndependence and choices over the services they receive.

ctices on disability and the assumptions accompanying
used controversy, not least among disabled people
paigns by disabled people have led to some modification
emes of discrimination against them. Policies have been
n that forbid many of the most apparent types of physical
ination, such as the failure of architects and designers
public buildings and dwellings which a person with a
king frame can enter and use.

h century, the direction of government policy on
of people with learning disabilities is indicated by
the White Paper *Valuing People* (DH, 2001a). It sets
the keywords of which are highlighted in bold below,
n service provision:

self-help groups or carers' organisations and groups may be necessary
and also telephone and internet contact numbers and addresses.

Even though ageing is often associated with growing vulnerability and the
older person's fears about being unable to cope, social workers, working
with other practitioners in health and social care, can develop with the
older person empowering strategies which can provide support and
maintain maximum independence.

SUMMARY

We have a growing proportion of older people in the population
because of people's increasing life expectancy, with the
consequence that many are suffering an increasingly lengthy
period of decline, infirmity and dependence on carers and
health and social services. Social work with older people is
invariably practised on a multiprofessional basis. This chapter
has illustrated how through such practice social workers can
make a significant difference to the quality of life of older people.

RECOMMENDED READING

A good source of ideas and information about work with older
people: Lymbery, M. (2007) *Social work with older people. Context,
policy and practice*, London: Sage Publications.

A very well researched and informed book about concepts,
policies and the practice of work with older people: Phillips, J.,
Ray, M. and Marshall, M. (2006) *Social work with older people* (4th
edn), Basingstoke: Palgrave.

WEB LINKS

Help the Aged is a useful source of information about older people's situation and policies
www.helptheaged.org.uk

A project founded by Help the Aged to combine the experience of researchers, agencies and the care sector to establish principles of good practice in care
www.myhomelife.org.uk/ProjectThemes.htm

This British Society for Research on Ageing promotes research into the causes and consequences of ageing
www.bbsrc.ac.uk

National Eating Disorder Information Center
www.nedic.ca

Charity providing care and information regarding Alzheimer's disease in particular and dementia in general
www.alzheimers.org.uk

ocial work with

Introduction

Social workers working with disa
both to ensure services are pro
also to challenge discriminato
and against disabled groups of
of policies and concepts and
of work with disabled people

Contexts for practice

A high proportion of the p
impaired or disabled and so
Physical disabilities – or in
learning disabilities can lea
societal attitudes that stign
them from certain activit
conditions or circumsta
a person and that may k
from access to commu
Impairment is the te
loss of function or cor
or activities. In order
the person comes firs
society disables them
'disabled person' is

The actual
known, but
six of the p
disability is
stigmatising
skills. More
extremely si
1.5 million. A
what a learni
name even o

Impairment an
social work ta

- Impaired an
  public and
- Impaired an
  giving them

Policies and pra
them have aro
themselves. Cam
in the worst extr
put into legislatio
and social discrin
to create offices,
wheelchair or wa

Policy changes

Since the late 20
meeting the needs
the publication of
out four principles,
which should gover

■ Meeting people's **civil rights**.
■ Ensuring people achieve maximum **independence** consistent with meeting their needs.
■ Ensuring people have **choice** over how they engage with meeting their own needs.
■ Ensuring all that is done fulfils the goal of developing the **inclusion** of disabled people.

Campbell's (2002a) discussion of inclusive schooling applies more widely to social care and social work. Campbell defines **inclusion** as the aim of reducing inequality through including people in activities in mainstream society. Inclusion is not only a personal goal for the individual, but also a social goal for society. This is because the onus is not on the individual disabled person to adjust to being socially included in different aspects of society; there must be changes so as to bring about three forms of equality:

■ of the circumstances where the disabled person is included
■ of the disabled person's participation
■ of the inclusive outcome of the disabled person's participation.

Campbell (2002a, p 12) makes the point that there is a need to take into account how both inclusionary and exclusionary processes operate at the level of the organisation as well as in society as a whole. It is important to engage families, communities and other agencies in generating inclusiveness in each setting. Ideally, each setting where disabled people are dealt with is a locally based community 'with an emphasis on shared values and local participation' (Campbell, 2002a, p 33).

Additionally, government policy has focused on making changes to the social security system and putting in place various measures to encourage disabled people to join, or rejoin, the workforce. This, it is argued, not only relieves the Exchequer (the 'purse' of money held by the country) but it should improve the self-esteem of disabled people and improve their inclusion in society.

Historically, disabled people were discriminated against, stigmatised and excluded from society. Physically impaired people and people with learning disabilities alike were often shut away in institutions for most of their lives. Until the late 20th century, there were few policies that gave them resources and services to enable them to live independently.

Disability movement

Since the 1970s, impaired people have campaigned collectively through pressure groups and social movements (see below) against the widespread view that the causes of their impairments are medically based and located wholly in their bodies. The disability movement is not as unified as this heading might imply. It is the label applied to campaigns by disabled people themselves, from the pressure group, the Disability Income Group, of the late 1960s, to the Disability Movement that spread from the 1970s to many western countries. Together, disabled people have had success in three main ways:

■ challenging the stigma of disability
■ criticising services and bringing about policy change
■ developing independence rather than autonomy and self-sufficiency.

In different ways, these concerted and independent movements by disabled people have contributed to independent living and person-centred support, and self-directed support becoming part of the vocabulary of policy and practice in services for disabled people. These expressions all relate to the government strategy of personalising people's services (see Chapter Five), which has major implications for disabled people.

Personalisation in services for disabled people has its roots in **person-centred planning** – a strategy introduced in the government White Paper *Valuing People* (DH, 2001a). Person-centred planning is similar to personalisation, in that it focuses on providing people with resources and services sufficient to support them in living as independently as possible and to exercise control and choice over their services. This may be done through **direct payments** using **individual budgets** (see Chapter Six for a discussion of these).

Pen picture

Lucy has a learning disability as well as a physical impairment that means she has restricted mobility and uses a wheelchair to go shopping from the ground floor sheltered flat in which she lives alone. Her social worker asked her three years ago if she wanted to volunteer for a pilot scheme (referred to in Carr, 2008, p 5) to personalise services through self-directed support. This has enabled Lucy to:

- control the kind of support she needs
- take a full part in agreeing what services she needs
- agree the kind of support her relatives and friends provide over and above services
- be responsible for allocating the resources for her support in any way she chooses.

Lucy is now proceeding to negotiate with her social worker an individual budget so that she can have control over the entire range of health and social care services which she receives, whether in the form of cash direct payments or in the form of services.

Pen picture

Anton is 14 and is affected by cerebral palsy. This is a non-progressive condition, the symptoms of which vary widely, and in his case is marked by him being unable to speak clearly or walk and experiencing involuntary muscle spasms (that is, spasms over which he has no control).

Legal basis for practice

The legal definition of a disabled person under Section 29 of the 1948 National Assistance Act is people who are 'blind, deaf or dumb or who suffer from mental disorder of any description and other persons ... who are permanently and substantially handicapped by illness, injury or congenital deformity or such other disabilities as may be prescribed by the Minister'. Many other Acts can be used by social workers to support the case for services for disabled people (see Table 8.1).

Table 8.1: Illustrations of legal provision for services for disabled people

1948 National Assistance Act	Duty for local authority to provide residential care
1970 Chronically Sick and Disabled Persons Act	Local authority to provide practical help for people with chronic impairments
1986 Disabled Persons (Services, Consultation and Representation) Act	Strengthens provisions of the 1970 Chronically Sick and Disabled Persons Act
1990 NHS and Community Care Act	Duty for social services to assess people's needs and where appropriate provide community care
1995 Disability Discrimination Act	Duty of public bodies, including local authority, to promote equality for disabled people
2006 Disability Discrimination Act	Duty of public bodies to promote equal opportunities for disabled people, eliminate discrimination and harassment of disabled people, promote participation by disabled people in social life
2006 Equality Act	Duty of public authorities to promote equality

Social workers, like many other practitioners in the health and social care sector, are responsible for upholding the rights of disabled people, advocating for them where necessary and ensuring that they are empowered to have access to the services they want, in order to meet their needs. The long list of legislation referred to in Table 8.1 is one indication that over the decades people with physical impairments and learning disabilities have been discriminated against and socially excluded, all of which has contributed to them, in effect, being disabled by society. The term **disablism** is often used to refer to attitudes and actions that express views and beliefs that disabled people are inferior to other people. The key legislation challenging discrimination against disabled people is the 1995 Disability Discrimination Act and its sequel, the 2006 Disability Discrimination Act. **Equality-based** policies are expressed in the 2006 Equality Act that led to the setting up of the Equality and Human Rights Commission, responsible for promoting equality in all aspects of people's lives.

Settings for practice

The many different settings in which disabled people have services include hospitals and residential homes, day services and centres and at home, where they may use their individual budgets to purchase the services of carers or personal assistants to enable them to live independently. The majority of health and social care services are commissioned by the NHS and local authorities and provided by voluntary and private organisations and groups. Increasingly, disabled people make their own choices and manage their own budgets, which means that they control the services delivered to them. The following two examples illustrate likely scenarios.

Example

Len has cerebral palsy and three years ago he negotiated with his social worker to change from receiving community care services to managing his own direct payments from the local authority adult care services department. He employs three part-time carers throughout the week on a rota. This enables him to fulfil his busy working and social life, largely split between attending meetings, running a local service user group and taking part in sports activities.

Example

Moira has a learning disability and employs a personal assistant three days a week to accompany her to meetings and to help her with clerical work. She tells her social worker she hates the term 'carer' and intends to use the term 'personal assistant' because it does not carry the stigma and does not make her sound as though she is dependent.

Approaches to practice

Models of disability and responses to disability

Disability is a generic word which refers to the social disablement of people who have physical impairments and/or who have learning disabilities. Services for people have tended in the past to be based on rather demeaning, stigmatising and discriminatory assumptions about their presumed 'deficits', 'abnormalities' and 'handicaps'. It is common to group together the different categories of these assumptions, so that the distinctions between them are evident. These are generally referred to as models of disability. A **model** is a set of ideas and assumptions that organises ideas about a topic.

Three main models of disability are evident in the large and ever-expanding volume of research reports, journal articles and books: medical, social and rights-based. To categorise them in this way does involve some simplification, but it is useful to draw the distinction between the models and approaches (see Table 8.2).

Individual model

This is sometimes called the 'biomedical model'. It assumes that the person's disability is a characteristic of them as an individual. It follows, therefore, that whether having physical impairment or learning disability, the person's condition is viewed like an illness, or at the very least as a departure from normality, which puts the person in the position of being

Table 8.2: **Models of disability**			
	Individual	Social	Rights
View of disability	Biomedical condition of the person	Disablement by social factors	Human rights
Responses by professionals	Treat the individual as the problem	Tackle social stigma and exclusion	Extend human rights

dependent and requires professionals to correct it (Barnes et al, 1999, p 25). Disability is viewed as a health defect, from a biomedical perspective.

Social model

From the viewpoint of the individual model, what the social model calls the disabling environment is assumed to be neutral. In contrast with this, the social model focuses on the extent to which a range of social structures and processes in various parts of society, such as housing, income, buildings, transport, education and employment, disable the person (Barnes et al, 1999, p 31). The 1970s and 1980s saw the rise of the social model, which rejected the medicalisation of the disablement of the person, inherent in the individual model. Wolfensberger (1972) proposed normalisation as an approach, starting from the viewpoint of non-disabled people, to respecting the qualities of disabled people and bringing their lives as close as possible to that of non-disabled people. Later Wolfensberger (1982) set out social role valorisation, which emphasised social devaluation and has been criticised for suggesting that non-disabled people should be treated inclusively in the mainstream rather than emphasising the importance of them associating with each other (Shakespeare, 2006, p 22).

Criticisms of the social model

Shakespeare (2006, p 2) makes many important points, among which the following three are vital. He:

■ rejects what he calls the 'strong social model approach to disability';

■ seeks a model which neither reduces disability to a medical problem nor neglects 'the predicaments of bodily limitations and difference';

■ argues that the social model has tended to over-emphasise the need for disabled people to be freed from disabling barriers which are socially based. He notes that the real impairments of people may require services as well. He draws the important distinction between independence and autonomy. Autonomy is a situation of complete separation from services, whereas independence is a recognition that some support is necessary. Independence is the term he prefers as a goal for disabled and impaired people.

Despite these criticisms, it remains certain that disabled people's rights have been advanced significantly through the progress made by many professionals and members of the general public, from the individual to the social model of disability.

Rights model

The rights model puts the disabled person in the situation of being (actually or potentially) active and independent. Rather than starting from the assumption that disabled people have needs, it bases practice on the assumption that their rights are paramount. It shifts the emphasis from the individual and the social factors that disable the person to the need for policy and legal measures which advocate and support disabled people's rights and entitlements.

Pen picture

Marc has severe learning disabilities and a mild autistic condition. He is 20 and lives with his lone-parent father in a rural location; at present, through the support of a local social worker, he controls his individual budget, although it is managed by Personal Services, a local not-for-profit company limited by guarantee, which uses the computer to act as a 'virtual' intermediary agency for service users who wish to have personalised health and social care services.

Marc's father negotiated a personal assistant for Marc, managed through Personal Services. This person helps Marc to stay involved with the day centre and art and music therapy sessions that he enjoys there.

Through balancing the risks to Marc against the benefits to him of remaining independent, the social worker continues to justify the personalised services Marc controls with his father, in terms of the opportunity they give Marc to remain independent. There are risks to his safety, but these are balanced against the clear evidence of Marc's enhanced health and well-being.

Practice

Social work with disabled people is not restricted to arranging aids and adaptations for them, important though this is. This is a rather historic view of the functions of social services, dating from the 1970s, when social services departments distributed mainly physical resources to physically impaired people under the 1970 Chronically Sick and Disabled Persons Act. In the 21st century it is still vitally important for people with serious impairments – they may be blind, deaf, unable to walk, or may suffer combined impairments – to have the benefits of assistive technology (adaptive rehabilitative and other devices to enable people to maximise their independence). A range of social work approaches and methods are used to enable and empower people to develop their capacity to live a fuller and more independent life, among which are counselling, advocacy and empowerment.

It is important for social workers to enable disabled people to advocate for themselves – the term **self-advocacy** is often used to refer to this. More generally, advocacy is a word most commonly used in legal settings, where it means different forms of representation for people. In social work, advocacy refers more often to the idea of lay people speaking up for each other, and in disability work the term self-advocacy is often used. It means putting forward a view about your own circumstances.

Self-advocates typically aim to empower themselves to take key decisions about the nature of services they need.

Pen picture

Michelle has a learning disability and she has a supporter, who is a volunteer who acts as her personal assistant, to enable her to continue to advocate on behalf of herself. Michelle's social worker, acting as facilitator, ensures that this arrangement continues, through Michelle's individual budget. The individual budget enables Michelle to specify what services she wants and how she wants them delivered. Michelle's supporter does the job but does not try to take over Michelle's decisions or reduce her independence. One of Michelle's aims is to continue with her membership, and on occasions chairing the local group of the voluntary agency organising the Supporters' Scheme. Michelle's supporter often helps her with the practical tasks associated with arranging and attending these meetings, as well as sitting next to her throughout the meetings and quietly whispering explanations of what is going on. Michelle has set up a system of red and green cards which disabled members of the group hold up at the meetings, either when they want to stop the business in order to clarify something (red card), or to say the business can go ahead (green card). Michelle's social worker ensures that Michelle's supporter has received training and still receives adequate supervision, to ensure that she carries out her responsibilities so as to empower Michelle and not overpower her. Michelle's training was funded by the local authority, but was led by a disabled person.

Michelle and her supporter tell her social worker frankly when they meet, not just about what is going well, but also about what is not going well. The social worker takes these critical comments as a compliment that they trust her to be able to absorb criticism, to reflect on it and to respond professionally.

Developing quality group care

Some people with learning disabilities live in residential accommodation, and experience what is sometimes called 'group care'. In theory, it should be possible to create a homely, caring, supportive yet empowering setting in group care, but practice, as research by Clement and Bigby (2010) shows, may be far less than ideal.

What can we learn from Clement and Bigby's research? It provides important indicators as to the ingredients of good group care, nine of which can be summarised from their research findings:

- clear policy goals and consistent management at policy level, across the service
- ensuring group homes fulfil the principles set out in the government's learning disability strategy (DH, 2001a), referred to earlier in this chapter
- appropriate leadership and stable staffing in the group care setting, with low staff turnover
- sufficient help and preparation for staff
- continuous accountability of staff
- prioritising the quality of life of the individual over other considerations
- ensuring practice provides homely, supportive group care
- ensuring people have a high level of engagement and participation in meaningful activities in their own group care, as they would in their own home
- continuous monitoring of practice.

Key issues

Social workers have to manage tensions in situations where people have complex needs and the outcomes are uncertain. In work with disabled people, the development of personalised services requires an individual budget that will supply resources and services to enable a person to meet their own needs.

Pen picture

Stella has a learning disability. Her social worker has contacted the brokerage team of the local authority – a voluntary organisation called Independent Living Advocacy – with the aim of offering Stella a broker who will help her to negotiate and plan the most appropriate individual budget to meet her needs. The broker starts work with Stella, after the local authority has decided that she is eligible for the services, and sets the resource allocation and the actual budget.

Stella and the broker discuss her needs, expectations, wishes and preferences in detail. Together they construct a plan that will meet her needs and are eligible for services and other resources. The social worker ensures that she:

- supports the broker in ensuring that Stella's individual budget can meet her needs;
- makes sure that the system of brokerage does not become institutionalised and inflexible, but remains open to Stella.

SUMMARY

This chapter has surveyed only a few of the many circumstances in which people with physical impairments or learning disabilities are stigmatised, discriminated against or socially excluded. Social workers have responsibility for enabling people who are socially disabled in these ways to be empowered to maintain their independence. Some prefer not to be identified as disabled whilst others develop their own services, using direct payments or an individual budget. For these reasons, social work with disabled people tends to adopt a social or a rights-based approach, both of which recognise the extent to which people are disabled in society, although from slightly different vantage points.

RECOMMENDED READING

A good, basic introduction to up-to-date and critical 'social' and sociological views of disablement and disability: Barnes, C., Mercer, G. and Shakespeare, T. (1999) *Exploring disability: A sociological introduction*, Cambridge: Polity Press.

A quite personal, but very readable, account of ideas and practices around advocacy and self-advocacy (that is, disabled people's own advocacy): Brandon, D. (1995) *Advocacy: Power to people with disabilities*, Birmingham: Venture Press.

A critique of what is known generally as the social model of disability, which also contains interesting material on debates about disability, eugenics and euthanasia: Shakespeare, T. (2006) *Disability rights and wrongs*, London: Routledge.

WEB LINKS

Foundation for Learning Disabilities, part of the Mental Health Foundation, supports and carries out research and encourages service development
www.learningdisabilities.org.uk

Archive of previously published material at the University of Leeds
www.leeds.ac.uk/disability-studies/archiveuk/

Centre for Disability Research. Archive of papers from previous conferences based at Lancaster University
www.lancs.ac.uk/cedr/

social work with mental health, illness and recovery

Introduction

Social workers are well placed, because of their particular multidisciplinary knowledge base and wide range of approaches and methods of working, to make a professional contribution to mental health services in a variety of settings, some of which are multiprofessional and may be based on joint working between the NHS and social work or social services agencies or departments of local authorities, or specialist agencies in the private, voluntary and independent sectors. The broad sociological as well as psychological social sciences base on which social workers draw ensures that social as well as clinical aspects of mental illness and people's mental health needs are taken into account, whether intervening in people's lives, or planning and delivering services with them.

Contexts for practice

The policy and organisational context for mental health services has changed markedly since the late 20th century. Services are provided by mental health trusts through local GPs, other primary healthcare providers or through specialist providers, using private, voluntary and independent agencies and organisations. There is a strong emphasis on provision through partnerships, between different organisations and professional groups and between these and service users and carers. The voice of the person experiencing mental health problems is heard with increasing clarity by the commissioners and providers of mental health services.

Researchers and pressure groups in mental health such as Mind (www. mind.org.uk) confirm that mental health problems can have drastic consequences for individuals and on the family; for example, when a young adult develops mental health problems, or when a lone parent suffering from depression experiences the double jeopardy of being unable to hold down a job and is then rejected by a future potential employer, through the stigma of being labelled as mentally ill. In this way, mental illness can affect family members other than the person suffering from the condition. The stigma attached to mental illness was identified by Goffman in the 1960s (Goffman, 1968a and 1968b) and endures in the 21st century (Thornicroft and Kassam, 2008).

Present-day mental health problems in society

Mental health problems affect a significant and probably only partly known proportion of the population, with only the more visible mental health problems becoming 'news', such as the tiny proportion of people with serious mental disorders who attack, and sometimes kill people in public places and, when convicted, add to the significantly high total of about 3,500 people with serious mental disorders in England alone, who, in 2007, were held in secure conditions. A variety of terms is used to describe different units of psychiatric care of patients, including high dependency, intensive care, extra care, special care, locked wards and psychiatric intensive care units. Overarching the system of secure facilities in England are the three secure hospitals – Ashworth, Broadmoor and Rampton – used to detain convicted offenders who have a mental disorder.

Although these events are isolated and random, they eclipse the equally disturbing statistics on other mental health problems. A significant proportion of children and adults experience mental health problems and in general the likelihood of women being diagnosed with a mental illness is higher but men are more likely to be admitted as mental health inpatients. Numbers are rising, with adult male admissions up from 8,673 per year in 1990 to 13,400 in 2003-04 and female adult admissions up in the same period from 8,908 to 11,400 (DH, 2005b, Table 1). For instance, in 2007, more than 5,300 adults and young people aged 15 and over committed suicide, three quarters of whom were men, a fairly constant proportion during the years 1991 to 2007 (Mind, 2007). In contrast, rates of depression and anxiety remain between one and a half to twice as high among women as among men (DH, 2002).

Historical perspective: from asylums for insane people to community care

The Great Confinement of the 18th and 19th centuries was so called because numbers of large 'asylums' – known today as mental hospitals – were built to house people with mental health problems, often for years at a time. During the latter half of the 20th century, there was a massive shift, beginning with the closing of most of the large mental hospitals, and a change to supporting people with mental health problems in the community. There were four main reasons for this (see Jones, 1972):

- the increasing cost of long-stay institutions;
- increasing pressure on governments by pressure groups, including organisations involving and controlled by former users of psychiatric services;
- the development of drugs to curb many symptoms of mental illness making it increasingly possible under legislation (1959 and 1983 Mental Health Acts) for people with mental health problems to be supported in the community;
- the development of psychiatric social work;
- growing public and professional concern about conditions in mental hospitals.

Practice shortcomings

The period since the 1960s has seen a succession of scandals and public inquiries into conditions in mental hospitals (HMSO, 1969, 1971, 1972, 1978) which has raised serious public and professional doubts about whether the widespread use of institutional methods of dealing with people with mental health problems could continue to be justified. At the same time, there were several incidents where discharged people with a mental disorder attacked members of the public and several of these incidents led to deaths of the victims (see, for instance, Ritchie, 1994). This raised public and professional fears that the process of discharging people was risky and support for discharged former patients in the community was less than adequate.

The Disability Rights Movement has become increasingly active in the mental health field since the late 20th century. Mental health policy and practice, as a consequence, has been influenced positively by the views of users of mental health services.

Approaches to practice

Models of mental health

The treatment of people with mental health problems has been carried out in many different ways, based on a variety of different theories and methods. These can be summarised, as shown in Table 9.1.

Table 9.1: Models of mental health problems and responses to them

Model	Views of problem	Focus	Response
Medical	Individual pathology	Mental illness	Medical, including drugs or surgery
Social	Mental health problem	Environmental	Provide range of social supports
Recovery	Mental health problem	Personal and social identity	Move towards empowered rights-based tactics
Deviance	Stigma	Social processes	De-stigmatise De-carcerate De-medicalise

From the late 18th century the medical professions increasingly dominated the treatment of mental health problems, which tended to be defined as mental 'illness', a situation that is regarded as unexceptional nowadays.

From the 1960s, there were various attempts, partly from within the psychiatric profession (Laing, 1990; Cooper, 2000), to challenge the dominance of the medically based psychiatric treatment of mental health problems.

From the 1970s, there were radical critiques arguing that mental illness was a myth (Szasz, 1970, 1990). Szasz argues that:

■ mental illness is a construction of society, that is, not a distinctive or real category of human activity;
■ responses to so-called mental illnesses by professionals such as psychiatrists and social workers are really consequences of moral judgements made by those professionals.

According to Szasz's argument, people who suffer from mental illness are treated like the witches of modern society, in the sense that they are labelled, stigmatised and in extreme cases excluded from society. From the 1960s, critics of the application by professionals of biomedical and individually based models in disability shared common ground with radical psychiatrists, this territory being discussed in detail by Sedgwick (1982). The outcome of radical psychiatries, however, was not as Sedgwick's book might have anticipated – their incorporation into psychiatric mainstream thinking and practice. On the contrary, their widespread denial of the illness base of psychotic conditions, for instance, marginalised them on the radical fringes of psychiatric practice.

Activism by survivors (former patients) of psychiatric treatment, largely in mental hospitals, grew from the 1970s. The movement of people on the receiving end of psychiatric services and who were critical of them is symbolised by Survivors Speak Out, an organisation founded in 1986 and campaigning actively on behalf of psychiatric patients. The National Survivor User Network (www.nsun.org.uk) brings together groups run by service users and survivors of mental health services.

Since the 1980s, self-help groups in mental health have flourished (Lindenfield and Adams, 1984). Such groups as Depressives Anonymous have followed a pattern established by other 'anonymous groups', on the lines of the iconic Alcoholics Anonymous. Paradoxically, social workers have often played a part in working with such self-help groups, particularly in mental health, typically playing a lead role in initiating a group, moving quite quickly to a facilitating role and finally to the position of letting the group alone (Adams, 1990).

Despite the growing weight of criticism of the excessive application of the medical model in mental health practice since the mid-20th century and the lack of research evidence concerning the effectiveness of psychoanalytic perspectives that 'blame' the family, there is still a tendency for some health professionals to rely on the medical model in mental health. One sign of progress, however, (see the deviance model, Table 9.1) has been the removal of homosexuality from mental health theories about 'disease' and 'treatment'. Before the 1970s, homosexuality was treated by many doctors as a disease and criminalised in the criminal justice system. The situation began to change in 1974, when it was removed from the category of psychiatric disorders. Gradually, over succeeding decades, being gay has been regarded less as a stigma and increasingly as an accepted social identity.

Legal basis for practice

The two main pieces of legislation governing mental health practice in social work are the 1983 and 2007 Mental Health Acts. Both Acts deal with issues of mental illness and disorder, but those associated with a person's inability to manage their personal affairs are dealt with under the 2005 Mental Capacity Act.

The 2007 Mental Health Act emphasises community treatments supervised by professionals such as social workers as a means of preventing people with mental health problems being trapped in the 'revolving door' of continual admission to mental hospital, by requiring them to accept the treatments. The Act also improves support for carers of people with mental health problems by specifying how they should be involved in constructing care plans for service users. Social workers have the dual responsibility of ensuring this happens while guarding against carers taking on the additional work of chaperoning the person with a mental health problem. Estimates of the numbers of young carers vary (see Chapter Four), but it is likely that more than a third of young carers – this means more than 50,000 at any one time – care for a person, probably a parent, with a serious mental health problem. Research indicates that a **young carer**, that is, a child or young person who cares for a parent or carer (in this case, with mental health problems) experiences isolation through avoiding social activities, partly as a result of the stigma attached to mental illness (Parrott et al, 2008).

The Mental Health Act Commission, which reviewed the working of the 1983 Mental Health Act with particular regard to the welfare and rights of patients detained under this Act, was responsible for reviewing the working of the 1983 Mental Health Act. It was abolished in 2009 and its functions absorbed into the new CQC.

National standards for mental health work

The government's national standards for mental health work (DH, 1999a, 1999c) set out standards summarised here:

■ Promoting mental health for all, tackling prevention of mental illness and combating discrimination against, and promoting inclusion of, individuals and groups with mental health problems.
■ Improving primary care, including the identification, assessment and effective treatment of mental health needs.
■ Providing accessible, round-the-clock services for people with common mental health problems and effective referral on to specialist services.
■ Providing all mental health service users with severe mental illness and who are on the care programme with a level of care which anticipates crises, reduces risks and gives them clear, written information about what to do in a crisis and how to access services at any time, 365 days a year.
■ Providing for all mental health service users assessed as needing to receive supervised medical care, timely access to a hospital or alternative accommodation in the least restrictive environment and as close to home as possible.

■ Providing for all carers of individuals on care programmes with written assessments of their own needs as carers, the implementation of which is to be discussed with them and reviewed annually.

The Child and Adolescent Mental Health Services (CAMHS) set out to meet the needs of children and young people. In 2008 these services were reviewed by the government with a view to ensuring that mental health should be regarded as the responsibility of all professionals working with children and young people and not simply left to specialist CAMHS workers. The involvement of children and young people (asking them about their experiences of services and their expectations of services, for instance) also was prioritised.

Roles for social workers doing mental health work

Social workers with people with mental health problems have to undertake additional (normally called post-qualifying) training after an initial period of practice following professional qualification. Approved social workers (ASWs) or approved mental health professionals (AMHPs) are qualified professionals, who in the case of the AMHPs have replaced the ASWs as a title, and could be either health professionals or social workers who have achieved a post-qualifying award in mental health practice. Early indications are that, far from either nurses or social workers monopolising the 'values' or the 'practices' of the programmes, both health and social perspectives are represented in the content of these post-qualifying programmes and nurses and social workers completing the programmes find the health and social perspectives equally challenging, from their own professional viewpoints (Hunter, 2009, p 26).

Social workers are well placed to make a significant contribution to multiprofessional settings such as community mental health resource teams and other integrated settings, although their titles and specific pathways to career progression may vary in different parts of the UK (see Table. 9.2).

Table. 9.2: **Social work roles and titles in mental health work**	
Practitioner	**Adviser/consultant**
Social work lead	Social work adviser
Social work team leader	Social work consultant
Senior practitioner	Mental health consultant
Senior social worker	Mental health specialist
Responsible clinician[a]	Clinical adviser (mental health)
Social worker	
Community mental health worker	

Note: [a] Responsible clinician is the term used to refer to the leadership role in a mental health setting. There is the potential for a social work professional to move to the specialist role of consultant social worker and beyond this to become a responsible clinician.

Social workers in mental health settings carry out integrated assessments, risk assessments, negotiate care plans with service users and other professionals, carry out treatment sessions such as individual, group or family therapy and contribute to reviews of people's care plans.

New Ways of Working

Concern about the practice implications of the contemporary expectations arising from the development of statements of standards expected of practice has led the government to anticipate what are the 'ten essential shared capabilities' – in professional language, these are the kinds of knowledge, understanding and skills – to be expected of mental health professionals (DH, 2004a).

A Department of Health programme under the heading of New Ways of Working (DH, 2007) deals with the provision of mental health services across the entire health and social care field as such, including social work. The programme applies to all health and social care professionals who contribute to providing mental health services. It began with the New Ways of Working for psychiatrists initiative that accompanied a report in 2005 (DH, 2005c), and was followed by the publication *New Ways of Working for all* in 2007 (DH, 2007).

The particular feature of the New Ways of Working approach is that tasks are shared democratically by members of the team (see Figure 9.1), rather than being allocated hierarchically, for instance, by the consultant psychiatrist as head of the team (see Figure 9.2).

Figure 9.1: Democratic team

Shared responsibilities decided by all team members

All team members

Figure 9.21: Hierarchical team

Responsibilities allocated by manager

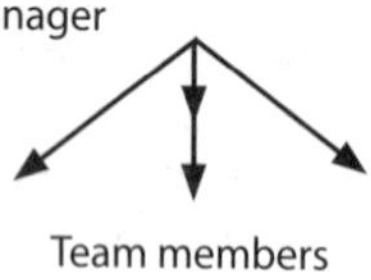

Team members

This approach (see Figure 9.1) intends to tackle the problems of insecurity and marginalisation experienced by some social care and social work professionals when entering a multidisciplinary mental health practice setting. Particular advantages of the New Ways of Working approach for social workers and other professionals include the possibility of acquiring new skills and perhaps moving into a specialist role as consultant social worker or a leadership role, as responsible clinician.

There is some way to go before mental health services in all parts of the UK achieve an ideal level of integration (Parrott et al, 2008). In some aspects of practice, the complexity of people's problems necessitates a cluster of approaches. For instance, **dual diagnosis** is a term that refers to the presence of both psychiatric (mental health) problems and drug misuse problems. People with both of these sets of problems are often very vulnerable and also experience unemployment, homelessness and social exclusion.

Post-qualifying practice

Social workers who undertake post-qualifying training after qualifying and gaining sufficient experience can become AMHPs. An AMHP can play a key role in taking decisions in specialist mental health practice and can make a significant contribution to the work of a multidisciplinary or integrated mental health team (see Chapter Eight).

Settings for practice

A range of agencies, organisations and groups provide mental health services, sometimes working individually and at other times in partnerships (see Figure 9.3).

Figure 9.3: Range of settings for delivery of mental health services

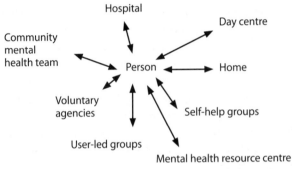

Pen picture

Meg is a social worker who facilitates self-help projects, starting up groups with people who suffer from various mental health problems. She attends groups at the start to facilitate them, then leaves once they become established.

Community care

Medication has made it possible for people with many chronic and potentially disabling mental disorders and conditions to live and work in the community.

Pen picture

David is schizophrenic. His social worker sometimes reminds him to continue to voluntarily attend an outpatients clinic once a fortnight to receive top-up medication. This keeps his symptoms under control and enables him to hold down his part-time job as a proofreader.

Child and adolescent mental health

Children suffer from a range of mental health problems and some of these are recognisably similar to those experienced by adults. For instance, childhood depression can be a serious and recurrent problem. The reasons for the changing incidence of childhood mental health problems are difficult to identify, as many young people are not in touch with the mental health services. For instance, although suicide rates among young people aged 10 to 19 in the UK appear to have declined by 28% between 1997 and 2003, it is true that three times the number of young men commit suicide as young women, yet we do not know why this has happened, since during this period only 14% of these young people were in touch with mental health services in the year before their death, in contrast with 26% of adults, and whereas 20% of young females were in contact, only 12% of young males who committed suicide were in contact (Windfuhr et al, 2008).

CAMHS is a multidisciplinary service, which means that a range of different professionals contributes to its work, including psychiatrists, psychiatric nurses, nurses, psychotherapists, psychologists and social workers. The service normally works with children who are up to 16 years old and their families. CAMHS normally accepts referrals from medical professionals in a range of settings (see Figure 9.4).

Approaches to practice

The approach adopted to particular types of mental illness depends on their nature, whether, for instance, they are based on a neurosis, a psychotic condition or a personality disorder. Some approaches are

Figure 9.4: Sources of referrals of child and family to CAMHS

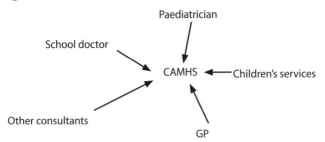

more clinical while others reflect social assumptions. Others again are developmental. For instance, we might regard it as logical where possible to build on the apparent links between children's mental health and the way they are brought up. Despite this, holistic (meaning a complete, whole-person or whole-family focus) approaches such as, but not only, family therapy, or whole-family approaches which bring together children's and adults' services, health and social services, including social work, are, as noted below, not that common. Despite this limitation, the richness and diversity of approaches and methods of working with children and adults with mental ill health is to be applauded. Social workers and others in multidisciplinary teams working with children and adults with mental health problems may develop, draw on and contribute to therapeutic work in many different traditions (see Figure 9.5).

Figure 9.5: Approaches to practice

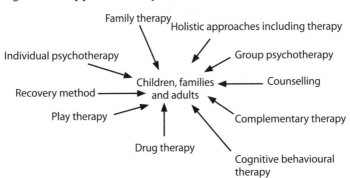

Cognitive behavioural therapy

The Human Givens strategy used in the Hartlepool branch of Mind involves combining a therapeutic approach such as cognitive behavioural therapy with the knowledge and skills that people already have, and working to enable them to tackle their problems. Human Givens are defined as certain attributes with which people are so familiar they take them for granted: 'needs, physical and emotional, and abilities, which enable people to meet those needs' (Taylor, 2009, p 29).

Counselling

People with mental health problems may respond to counselling approaches, which may be combined with other approaches, such as drug therapy.

Drug therapy

Drugs have been used increasingly since the last quarter of the 20th century as a means of treating people with mental health problems. Advances in the availability of drugs are largely responsible for this trend.

Family therapy

Family therapy remains a significant method of treatment of mental health problems and this is a specialism in which some social workers train. Some practise in multidisciplinary settings, such as outpatient clinics at hospitals, or in adolescent mental health facilities.

Other therapeutic approaches

A great variety of therapeutic approaches are adopted in work with people with mental health problems, varying from individual and group psychotherapy, play therapy with children and a range of complementary therapies.

Holistic approaches

Holistic approaches have two components:

- they focus on the patient as a whole and not just on the mental health symptoms of the patient;
- they work with the patient in the wider context of relationships, family, schools, work and community.

Holistic work with people can also be preventive as well as remedial (that is, only beginning after the symptoms, condition or illness have appeared). Research (Aldridge, 2002) shows that where agencies and professionals only provide services to the person with the mental health problem, this increases the stigma and also excludes other people in the household or family support network from benefiting from services and associated support. The alternative is to develop an holistic approach to working with the family and, hopefully, develop sufficient resources with them to prevent the problems of stigma and isolation often associated with mental illness overwhelming either individuals or other family members. Despite the necessity for more joined-up services, by no means do all UK mental health services offer a whole-family, or holistic, approach (Parrott et al, 2008).

Practice

There is a wide span of practices, geared to meeting the needs of people suffering from phobias (for instance, agoraphobia means a fear of open spaces), depression and neurotic conditions towards one end of the continuum and major mental disorders at the other.

Recovery approaches

The concept of recovery remains controversial in the mental health field, since it could be regarded as inextricably linked with the medical model of treatment. In reality, recovery means many different things and there is no single definition of it. It can mean restoring the person to complete health, or it can mean gaining control over one's circumstances.

Crisis resolution and **home treatment** are terms used to refer to recovery-oriented methods that provide opportunities for a more personalised way of responding to people's mental health needs.

Recovery methods may offer alternatives to the medical model of diagnosis and clinically based treatment. They can be akin to a self-help approach in that they emphasise the strengths and experiences of the individual rather than putting his or her mental health problems at the centre (Repper and Perskins, 2003). The Recovery International Method (www.lowselfhelpsystems.org), for instance, is allied to the 12-step approach of Alcoholics Anonymous, and relates the progress of the person to taking control and to the development of will power to overcome problems. Recovery International (www.recovery-inc-ireland. ie) is a self-help organisation based in Ireland that enables the person to develop techniques to control temperamental tendencies and behaviour. The Mental Health Foundation (2008) publishes useful information on recovery approaches. Further information about recovery approaches is given in the 'Web links' at the end of this chapter.

Assertive community treatment and assertive outreach

Assertive community treatment is a term used for assertive community-based approaches. As used in the US, it is a very structured approach that can be as reliant on the use of drugs to control undesirable behaviour as institutionally based treatments. **Assertive outreach**, discussed by Ryan and Morgan (2004), is a strengths-based approach, based on the assessment of people's strengths and building this into the care planning and coordination.

Pen picture

Lisa is 16, and is trying to complete her GCSEs at school. She has a secret she shares with few people outside the family. She is one of upwards of 50,000 children and young people in the UK – most of whom are girls – who care for a parent or other close relative in the household – most often the mother – with a mental health problem. Lisa's mother suffers from unpredictable episodes of depression and this makes it difficult for Lisa to keep her focus on school. Typically for children in her situation, Lisa feels stigmatised by her mother's problem and does not mix with other children, or have children home to play.

Fortunately, Lisa's caring responsibilities have recently become known to local children's services. Her social worker knows how crucial it is to offer a whole-family approach, rather than a patient-led approach, through three kinds of support and services, to:

- Lisa, to enable her to start living a fuller social life, as well as engaging more positively with school and reaching her full potential;
- Lisa's mother, so that Lisa's caring burden is shared with different services and professionals as appropriate, without stigma to her or other family members;
- other members of the family.

Admission to low, medium or high security facilities

Social workers play a key role in those circumstances where people need to be admitted to mental hospitals, on a compulsory basis. **Psychiatric intensive care** is the term used for patients who are detained compulsorily in secure conditions, usually where they are suffering from acute (short-term) symptoms of a mental disorder. **Sectioning** is a term often used to refer to the process of using the law to detain someone in a mental hospital under the 1983 Mental Health Act. This is a reference to the use of particular sections of the legislation (Section 2: admission for assessment; Section 3: admission for treatment; Section 4: emergency admission; and Section 5: compulsory detention of an informal patient already in hospital).

Discharge from hospital

Social workers are generally involved when a person is discharged from hospital, after being detained for treatment under the 1983 Mental Health Act. Section 117 requires that they receive free services, without the means testing which often would accompany the provision of adult social care services. Social workers are well placed to ensure that these decisions are made appropriately by local authorities.

Pen picture

Mr Jones is 80 and has been in hospital for several weeks with a broken leg. He is discharged and his social worker makes sure that his wishes have been met and he is to be discharged to his sheltered flat, with a carer visiting morning and night to help him with washing and dressing and personal hygiene, personal care and other domiciliary services (personal care is wider than personal hygiene; see Chapter Five). The social worker makes sure that Mr Jones is not means tested for these services, which should be provided free under Section 117 of the 1983 Mental Health Act.

Key issues

Social work practice in mental health remains dominated by notions of risk management and the tension between professionally led practice and service user-based services.

Risk management

In mental health policy and practice, the highlighting of occasional incidents in the mass media, where a person with a severe mental health disorder commits an act of criminal violence, perpetuates the stigmatisation of many people with less serious mental health problems. It also leads to much practice being dominated by the assessment and management of risks of harm, partly to the service user, but largely to other members of the public, if the person continues to receive treatment and support in the community. In this way, the notion of risk can override more sophisticated and subtle aspects of practice. The care programme approach has developed over the past decade (DH, 1999b) to support people with more serious mental disorders.

Service user participation

The principle of service user involvement is central to practice. However, there is a tension between the traditional mental health services based on professionals assessing people and delivering treatment, and the 21st-century prospect of service users developing their own plans for their mental health services, based on their self-assessments of their circumstances. This view of the future becomes more real since the mid-1990s, when direct payments to service users became a reality and since 2000, when the personalisation agenda gathered momentum and made individual budgets possible.

However, we need to temper these possibilities with realism. Research indicates that the take-up of direct payments by service users with mental health problems is lower than for other groups, some of the problems lying in the impact of reorganising services on the workloads of professionals, including social workers (Ray et al, 2008).

SUMMARY

Mental illness affects people throughout childhood and adulthood. Many mental health problems are not simply 'illnesses', caused solely by physiological (that is, hereditary or biological) factors, but originate partly in social circumstances, such as poverty, poor housing and social isolation.

Social work applies a generic framework for responding to mental illness and this places social workers in a good position to develop multidisciplinary and multiprofessional approaches to working with people with mental health problems.

RECOMMENDED READING

Gives a detailed and authoritative picture of the realities of the experiences of young carers for people with mental health problems: Aldridge, J. and Becker, S. (2003) *Children caring for parents with mental illness: Perspectives of young carers, parents and professionals*, Bristol: The Policy Press.

A relevant discussion of mental health policies, models and practice: Glasby, J. and Lester, H. (2006) *Mental health: Policy and practice*, Basingstoke: Palgrave.

A basic sourcebook illustrating contemporary legal and professional aspects of mental health relevance to social work: Golightley, M. (2008) *Social work and mental health* (3rd edn), Exeter: Learning Matters.

Ryan, T. and Pritchard, J. (eds) (2004) *Good practice in adult mental health*, London: Jessica Kingsley Publishers.

WEB LINKS

Information and campaigns on mental illness and health, from Mind, a leading mental health charity
www.mind.org.uk

Mental Health Foundation: organisation promoting the quality of life of people with mental health problems or learning disabilities
www.mentalhealth.org.uk

10
social work with groups and communities

Introduction

Social workers are engaged in working with people, as individuals and in families. This chapter deals with aspects of social work that involve working with any of these, in group work and in communities or with a community focus. These ways of practising cut across the different client groups because they represent a different domain of intervention to working with individuals – a distinctive feature of social work is the capacity to respond to the collective as well as to the personal aspects of people's needs. Work with communities also entails work with groups, that is, groups in the community or community groups. This simple statement is the basic connection between these two in this chapter – group work and work with communities.

Social work with groups

Group work offers the practitioner an extra dimension for practice and to the client it also offers the opportunity to share problems and issues with other people. Group work can be empowering both for the practitioner and for the other members of the group. Some groups are led by practitioners, while others are led by service users and carers. Stanton (1990, p 122) has researched social services agencies such as advice centres, law centres and women's refuges, and suggests that in such situations the practitioner needs to be able to challenge the status quo in agency practices and be confident and assertive enough to support people using those services in their efforts to empower themselves, for instance, in advocating for themselves (the term used for this is 'self-advocacy').

For both practitioner and client, a group can be a way out of the confinement and isolation of dealing with problems alone. Group work is a means by which the client can be empowered, first, by sharing experiences and second, by learning from other people new ways of tackling problems. In the process, the relationship between the practitioner and the client has the potential to become more democratic, since the clients now outnumber the professional.

Consciousness-raising and conscientisation

One consequence of experiencing a group will also be relevant when we consider work with communities in the second part of this chapter, namely that the individual's awareness of the personal and social situation is enhanced – a process generally known as **consciousness raising**. The results of this may be very dramatic, whether the person experiences an 'Aha!' moment of enlightenment or a gradual process of becoming more aware. The writer about this process I find most stimulating and exciting, even 30 years after first reading his books in the early 1970s, is the activist Paulo Freire. Freire (1986 [1972], p 15), in his book *Pedagogy of the oppressed*, first published in 1972, uses the term **conscientisation** to refer to 'learning to perceive social, political and economic contradictions, and to take action against the oppressive elements of reality'. Thus, the concept refers to the process of making connections between one's personal circumstances and issues in the wider world. Freire engaged in work with poor people, to raise their awareness and confidence to the point when they could challenge their dependence and powerlessness and, potentially, overcome their economic, cultural, intellectual and emotional oppression. Freire describes this as a humanising process, an educational process involving people developing a deepening historical awareness of their situation, thereby acquiring the capacity to intervene and change their lives (Freire, 1986, pp 80-1). He explains how they need to take part in this process with a growing awareness of their contribution to the transformation as subjects. This is quite a difficult word to appreciate, out of its context, but basically what he means is that they need to be in control, rather than remaining dependent on, or controlled by, others. If they are not in control, the oppressors will still retain part control inside their heads, leading to them only imagining they have acquired power to change their situation. They may even be misled into collaborating in the 'installation of bureaucracies which undermine the revolution.... They may aspire to revolution as a means of domination, rather than as a road to liberation' (Freire, 1986, pp 97-8). Rather than being put off by the way Freire uses the word 'revolution', we should think of this as 'transformation'. What he is writing does not then lose its impetus, and at the same time becomes compatible with the terms used in contemporary UK health, social and other public services policy, infused with the government's commitment to transform them.

Contexts

Some commentators (such as Ward, 2009, p 115) are pessimistic about what they see as the decline of group work in social work, but others remain upbeat. Social workers, often working with other professionals such as youth workers and workers in voluntary organisations, still rely on work with groups of children, young people and adults in particular aspects of their practice, including work with families as groups and work with people experiencing a wide range of problems.

Defining group work

A **group** is defined as three or more people who interact together and are perceived by themselves and others as sharing experiences. **Group work** is the general term applied to a variety of approaches to working with and within groups to bring about change. The family is a type of group and social workers who work over a period of time with all the members of a household, or a cluster of relatives, could be said to be working with the family as a group. Again, there are so-called **group care** settings such as a day centre or residential home, and sometimes the social worker works with a group of people over a period of time in one of these settings. Yet again, a social worker may do therapeutic work alongside therapists – such as art, drama or music therapists – with a group of illicit drug takers, or former victims of abuse. Finally, a social worker may facilitate a group of people – such as people with mental health problems – setting up and running their own self-help group. These groups are commonly known as self-help or user-led groups. Informal (that is, unpaid, as opposed to those who are employed by an agency or, indeed, paid by the service user from a direct payment) carers are well organised and nowadays there are many groups and organisations of carers.

Self-help groups engage in five main types of activity, according to Tracy and Gussow (1976, p 382): therapeutic, social, educational, research and community action. There are three main types of relationship (Adams, 2008b, pp 119-20) between such groups and professional social workers: integral, facilitated and autonomous. **Integral** self-help is at first sight a contradiction in terms. It includes initiatives such as an independence or self-help unit, which may have the term 'self-help' in its title, run by clients or service users as part of a professionally run service; **facilitated** self-help is where social workers do certain things to enable the group, for example, to organise somewhere to meet and attend the occasional meeting to give input, such as demonstrating how to use group activities to tackle particular issues; **autonomous** self-help includes groups controlled and run completely independently of professionals.

Approaches to group work

Many different approaches may be associated with group work and a search on the internet will soon reveal a variety of uses of the term that may be bewildering for the newcomer. Groups can be categorised in terms of three main types of approach: problem-focused; development; and awareness raising. The variety of **problem-focused groups** can potentially include every form of therapy, helping and self-help. The latter is important since a great range of self-help groups exists alongside professionally led groups. Development includes **educational and personal development groups**, such as personal growth and adult education. Awareness raising includes what is often referred to as **consciousness-raising groups**, heightening people's knowledge and understanding of a topic or issue, perhaps leading to them taking some form of social action.

Practising group work

Qualifying programmes in social work often contain modules on group work, which students can undertake as specialist options. After qualification, some social workers specialise in work where group approaches are appropriate, such as sex offenders, drug and alcohol abusers and people with mental health problems.

Stages in the 'life' of a group

Methods of group work commonly take account of widely established knowledge about the 'natural' tendency of groups to go through a series of stages during their life cycle. These have been described in various ways by different commentators:

- forming: being set up
- storming: working through the process of members interacting and sorting out their relative power relations
- norming: establishing rules and agreeing working procedures
- performing: reaching the point where the group can get on with its tasks
- adjourning: reaching an end point, perhaps where members review progress and move on.

Some groups are facilitated by social workers rather than led by them and this is particularly the case with groups led and controlled by service users and carers. Self-help groups fall broadly into this category; they are groups set up by people experiencing a problem or shared issue, to enable them to tackle it themselves.

Running a group

There are many books on group work (Whitaker, 1985; Preston-Shoot, 1987; Douglas, 1993) that discuss how to plan, set up and maintain a group, and each of them emphasises slightly different aspects. Some of the unavoidable issues are very practical, such as deciding on a focus, finding enough members, finding a place to meet and ensuring sufficient basic resources to continue meeting (such as paying for the room and providing basic refreshments such as a hot or at least a cold drink). Other aspects include ensuring that the group is adequately led, such as ensuring that conflict between members can be dealt with if and when it arises and ensuring that the ending of the group is dealt with. Endings can be as difficult to manage as beginnings, and two ways of avoiding the issue are either to run an open-ended group, with people joining and leaving while the group continues, or to decide at the start that the group will run for, say, 12 weeks, two hours a week with a short comfort break in the middle of each meeting, so everybody knows that towards the end of that 12-week period there is no uncertainty about the group winding down.

Social work with communities

Defining work with communities

There is a great range of work with communities, which means that this area of practice is difficult to define. On the one hand, it could simply mean any service provided by the local authority *for* the community. On the other hand, it could mean community development facilitated by the worker but very definitely led and controlled by local residents *in* the community. **Community development** is a general term used to refer to a variety of community-based practice and it is important to distinguish this from community liaison or coordination. Liaison and coordination, like partnership, are terms that refer to joint working, whereas community development implies working for change. One aspect all work with communities shares is that it is to a greater or lesser extent political in nature. That is, it is concerned with the supply of resources to meet people's needs. Stepney and Popple (2008, p 115) refer to this as the target of intervention being the service user's social network, rather than the service user. Included in this network are the organisations that manage and deliver services.

There is debate about whether social workers can 'do' community work, that is, as community workers. Irrespective of our views about it, it is the case that all social work takes place *in* communities, but that social work *with* communities receives relatively little attention in textbooks about social work, in contrast, say, with child protection or disability.

Twelvetrees (2008) discusses different types of community work, from working with neighbourhood groups, through working with voluntary agencies in the not-for-profit sector and getting involved in communities and engaging in neighbourhood regeneration.

Contexts of work with communities

During the 1960s and 1970s, community work was a developing specialism and some local authorities and voluntary agencies employed community workers who were often based in a particular neighbourhood with a brief to enable members of the local community, working together, to develop community action around issues which concerned local people. In the late 1960s, community development projects were initiated by the government, focusing on issues such as the promotion of advocacy and welfare rights, in half a dozen localities throughout Britain.

During the subsequent decades, community action, whether led by paid local authority employees or by workers from neighbourhood or voluntary organisations, declined. It proved difficult for professional community workers to manage the tension between being employees of the state (through their employment by the local authority) and being accountable to local residents to promote their interests, perhaps by helping them to mount a campaign on an issue, 'against' that same local authority. Community work, as an activity, became increasingly one of a number of terms such as 'community liaison', 'community regeneration', 'community care' and 'community-based', which were used more widely. To some extent, this proliferation both muddled and diluted the field of community development, in the sense that it was now quite common and acceptable for workers to engage in practice 'in the community' rather than for community work to engage local people as activists or in campaigns which they initiated and owned.

Since the 1990s, there has been a growing number of policy initiatives led by governments, with the aim of stimulating community development, under such headings as 'community regeneration' and 'regional development'.Twelvetrees (2008, pp 200-7) contrasts policy-led initiatives with local grassroots-led, so-called 'bottom-up' approaches.

Approaches to work with communities

There is not one simple approach to working with a community, but many different approaches. These can be categorised in terms of the different levels at which the work is developed.We can view this from the vantage point of the practitioners or, more appropriately given the focus of community practice with empowering people to mobilise resources, from the vantage point of people themselves. Research by Saegert and Winkel (1996), for instance, into housing cooperatives identifies four different levels at which people feel the benefits of empowering practice: the individual level, the group level, the quality of life in the building level (which we could call the level of the organisation) and the community level, that is, the extent to which people's participation in community activities increases.Twelvetrees (2008, pp 3-7) identifies several different dimensions of community work:

- neighbourhood or community development work versus a planned approach, where workers facilitate local people achieving their collective goals, as opposed to local professionals taking a lead;
- self-help in the community versus a service, such as a lunch club organised by a group of residents rather than by the local authority;
- generic versus specialist community work, depending on whether work is done by a single worker with a single group of people, such as Women's Aid;
- process versus product groups, depending on whether those involved attach more value to the quality of the experience or the outcome;
- facilitating versus organising, depending on whether the work advises or takes the lead;
- community work as the worker's main job versus community work as an approach that can be undertaken by any local person;
- paid versus unpaid community work, which, as it sounds, distinguishes the paid worker from the unpaid volunteer or local activist.

Practice with communities

Effective work with communities depends on clarity at the outset about what is to be undertaken. It is also important to ensure that the necessary resources – finance, somewhere to meet, the appropriate people with the necessary skills – are available. Assuming these aspects are tackled satisfactorily, and accepting that every piece of community practice is unique and has its own particular characteristics, we can identify some general stages of a typical piece of work with a specific community of people:

1. Focus: considering possible areas for community practice
2. Meeting people: discussing with people in the community (local residents) their experiences and wishes
3. Sharing: identifying a short list of ideas and prioritising
4. Developing shared proposal: developing with residents a proposal jointly owned by the membership
5. Establishing the community project or intervention: making sure the practicalities of resourcing and where to meet are in place as the practice 'lifts off'
6. Collecting information: sharing with residents the task of collecting necessary information
7. Analysing: undertaking with residents the interpretation of the information
8. Implementing: carrying out the project
9. Evaluation: critically appraising with residents the achievements of the project and what remains to be done

At this point, the residents engaged in the project in the local community may decide that further work is necessary. This leads to a further series of activities, from stage 4 through to stage 9, and so on.

This is a summary of what may be a more complex process, but it gives an indication of the distinctive nature of collaborative work with local residents in community practice.

Networking

Networking is often mentioned in books on community practice of various kinds. A **network** is an arrangement of relationships between people who are connected by virtue of such bonds as where they live, friendship links, ties as relatives, common occupations or leisure activities. Practitioners working with children or adults may identify particular networks as of potential help to people in need. For instance, an isolated lone parent who is pregnant may benefit from being put in touch with a group of pregnant women from the locality.

Pen picture

Brenda, a lone parent, visits the children's centre in Blogtown and in the third month of her pregnancy is clearly struggling with her first child, seven months old, who is teething. A social worker, children and family support workers and a community nurse at the centre run a number of groups with mothers between them, covering the entire span from pregnancy through to the pre-school years. The groups tend to be small and reasonably self-contained, so that each one runs through the entire process, rather than one large group being open-ended.

Brenda is doubtful but is persuaded to attend one group meeting and after that she finds the group invaluable and becomes a regular attender. During that period, she draws on the resources of the group and the centre, to meet her needs and those of her growing family.

The group acts as a resource and begins to collect information on what is lacking and what is needed by parents in the locality, to meet their needs and those of their infants and young children. Members of the group, over time, join policy and management groups in the borough. The information they provide is incorporated into the services provided through the local children's plan of children's services for the borough.

Community profiling

A **community profile** is a widely respected way of gathering information about a community, that uses participatory means (that is, professionals working collaboratively, on an equal basis, with community members rather than doing things for them or to them) as the basis for action. The process of community profiling entails a group of people meeting to prepare and carry out the tasks of gathering information, analysing it and deciding together how to use the results.

Community capacity building

Community capacity building is 'the means by which communities build on their existing knowledge, skills and expertise and develop so as to meet the needs and priorities perceived as necessary by community members' (Adams, 2008b, p 161). Community capacity building overlaps with community development in the techniques used, but is different in the sense that whereas community development usually engages people in using skills from within the community, community capacity building often draws in expertise from outside the community, for instance, to give a particular initiative a kickstart.

SUMMARY

A particular strength of social work is that it is naturally positioned between different other professions working with people and the way it draws knowledge and understanding from law and the breadth of social policy, psychology and sociology. Social workers are able to make connections between different domains of people's lives, to develop different ways of understanding their problems and to use a diversity of approaches to working with them. For these reasons, social workers are well placed to work in partnerships that extend across organisations and a range of professions in such areas as education, health and social services.

RECOMMENDED READING

Two useful chapters, one on empowering work with groups, the other on empowering work with communities: Adams, R. (2008) *Empowerment and participation in social work*, Basingstoke: Palgrave, chapters 6 and 8.

A stimulating and ground-breaking book on consciousness-raising work with people: Freire, P. (1986 [1972]) *Pedagogy of the oppressed*, Harmondsworth: Penguin.

A very exciting, and challenging, book about community work: Ledwith, M. (2005) *Community development: A critical approach*, Bristol: The Policy Press.

A reliable basic book on community work: Twelvetrees, A. (2008) *Community work* (4th edn), Basingstoke: Palgrave.

A good book on group work: Whitaker, D.S. (1985) *Using groups to help people*, London: Tavistock/Routledge.

WEB LINKS

Promoting involvement of children and young people
www.hbr.nya.org.uk/HearbyRight

Shaping Our Lives: the national network of service users. An independent organisation advocating service user involvement
www.shapingourlives.org.uk/

Information from INVOLVE on promoting public involvement in health and social care
www.involve.org.uk/userempowerment

postscript

This book has attempted to convey the importance of the contribution social workers make to society. The reforms following from the Social Work Task Force (2009b) report are likely to enhance the benefits to people who use social services, as well as their carers, through raising the standards expected of social workers and improving the status of the profession, supervision and service delivery.

Social work is on the cusp of changes in society and in public services. Social workers are well positioned not only to respond, but also to contribute, to these changes. Students and practitioners alike will find social work at the forefront of changes in public services and playing a major part in ensuring people receive more personalised services. This depends on social workers ensuring that the connections between the different services – community, criminal justice, education, health, housing, leisure and social services – are made more effectively. It also depends on the development of more services that people design and manage themselves, tailored by them to meet their own needs.

Social work has a lengthy history in the UK, in its philanthropic casework rooted in the mid-19th century and, in its origins in mutual aid and self-help, much earlier than this. In many ways, however, the strength of the social work profession lies in the ability of practitioners to reinvent it, to meet people's needs in the modern world. In this sense, social work is a young profession.

Social workers are well placed, perhaps uniquely so among other professionals in the public services, to empower people not just to tackle their own problems but to enhance relationships with others, strengthen families and family support and build more cohesive and vital neighbourhoods and communities. Social work is a multifaceted profession that can enhance all of these domains of people's lives.

Social work practice is necessarily critical and social workers need to be sceptical, assertive and courageous. This follows from the twin realities that social workers draw on the social sciences, particularly sociology and social policy, and inevitably make connections between people's circumstances and problems such as poverty and other social inequalities and injustices, as well as abuse and violence involving children, vulnerable adults and – in the case of criminal violence in the home – between men and women. It is impossible for social workers to ignore the case for social and policy changes to challenge such social injustice and to ask themselves what personal and professional responsibility they should exercise as a consequence. It remains the case that research may illuminate these problems, but does not offer facile answers to them. So, the role of social workers is to be contributors to critical debates rather than to fantasy solutions – a very challenging role to perform.

Social work is unfinished. This is a consequence of the necessity for social work to change, in the wider context of social changes and changes in public services. New practitioners coming into social work bring new knowledge and understanding and new areas of expertise. They also bring enthusiasm. All of these are vital ingredients in reshaping social work.

Social workers are engaged in the task of enhancing their own practice. The process of becoming a social worker is never-ending, in the sense that once qualified, the practitioner is likely to seek opportunities for further personal and professional development.

The purpose of this book has been to open up this process and share it with the new entrant to social work. There is the prospect that it will become for you, the reader, as it has for me, stimulating, creative yet challenging, in the light of the complex problems people face in situations of change and uncertainty in the modern world.

references and further reading

Acheson, D. (1998) *Independent Inquiry into Inequalities in Health*, London: The Stationery Office.

Adams, R. (1990) *Self-help, social work and empowerment*, London: Macmillan.

Adams, R. (1991) *Protests by pupils: Empowerment, schooling and the state*, Brighton, Falmer.

Adams, R. (1992) *Prison riots in Britain and the US*, Basingstoke, Macmillan .

Adams, R. (1998) *The abuses of punishment*, Basingstoke, Macmillan.

Adams, R. (ed) (2007) *Foundations of health and social care*, Basingstoke: Palgrave.

Adams, R. (2008a) 'Basic needs', *International Encyclopedia of the Social Sciences*, William A. Darity, Jr (ed) vol 5 (2nd edn), Detroit, MI: USA Macmillan Reference, pp 455-6.

Adams, R. (2008b) *Empowerment, participation and social work*, Basingstoke: Palgrave Macmillan.

Adams, R. (2002) *Social policy for social work* , Basingstoke, Palgrave

Adams, R. (2010) *Foundations of complementary therapies and alternative medicine*, Basingstoke, Palgrave.

Adams, R. and Sawdon, D. (1979) 'In and out of work', *Actions*, January, pp10-13.

Adams, R., Dominelli, L. and Payne, M. (eds) (2009a) *Social work: Themes, issues and critical debates* (3rd edn), Basingstoke: Palgrave Macmillan.

Adams, R., Dominelli, L. and Payne, M. (eds) (2009b) *Critical practice in social work* (2nd edn), Basingstoke: Palgrave Macmillan.

Adams, R., Dominelli, L. and Payne, M. (eds) (2009c) *Practising social work in a complex world* (2nd edn), Basingstoke: Palgrave Macmillan.

Adams, R., Allard, S., Baldwin, J. and Thomas, J. (1981) *A measure of diversion? Case studies in intermediate treatment*, Leicester, National Youth Bureau.

Agnew, E. (2004) *From charity to social work: Mary E. Richmond and the creation of an American profession*, Chicago, Il: University of Illinois.

Aldridge, J. (2002) *Children caring for parents with severe and enduring mental illness*, Loughborough: Loughborough University.

Aldridge, J. and Becker, S. (2003) *Children caring for parents with mental illness: Perspectives of young carers, parents and professionals*, Bristol: The Policy Press.

Allen, C. (2007) *Crime, drugs and social theory: A phenomenological approach*, Aldershot: Ashgate.

Arksey, H., Hepworth, D. and Qureshi, H. (2009) *Carers' needs and the Carers' Act: An evaluation of the process and outcome of assessment*, York: SPRU.

Banks, S. (2006) *Ethics and values in social work* (3rd edn), Basingstoke: Palgrave.

Barnes, C., Mercer, G. and Shakespeare, T. (1999) *Exploring disability: A sociological introduction*, Cambridge: Polity Press.

BASW (British Association of Social Workers) (2002) *The code of ethics for social workers*, Birmingham: BASW.

Bazalgette, J. (1971) *Freedom, authority and the young adult*, London: Pitman.

Belsky, J., Barnes, J. and Melhuish, E. (eds) (2007) *The national evaluation of Sure Start: Does area-based early intervention work?*, Bristol: The Policy Press.

Biestek, F.P. (1961) *The casework relationship*, London: Allen & Unwin.

Black, D. (1980) *Inequalities in health*, London: Department of Health and Social Services.

Bradshaw, J. (1972) 'A taxonomy of social need', *New Society*, March, pp 640-3.

Bradshaw, J., Mayhew, E., Dex, S., Joshi, H. and Ward, K. (2005) 'Socioeconomic origins of parents and child poverty', in S. Dex and H. Joshi (eds) *Children of the 21st century*, Bristol: The Policy Press, pp 71-107.

Brandon, D. (1995) *Advocacy: Power to people with disabilities*, Birmingham: Venture Press.

Brandon, D. and Jordan, B. (ed) (1979) *Creative social work*, Oxford: Blackwell.

Braye, S. and Preston-Shoot, M. (2009) 'Social work and the law', in R. Adams, L. Dominelli and M. Payne (eds) *Social work: Themes, issues and critical debates* (3rd edn), Basingstoke: Palgrave Macmillan, pp 90-102.

Brayne, H. and Carr, H. (2008) *Law for social workers* (10th edn), Oxford: Oxford University Press.

Buckner, L. and Yeandle, S. (2007) *Valuing carers: Calculating the value of unpaid care*, London: Carers UK.

Butler, I. and Drakeford, M. (2006) *Scandal, social policy and social welfare* (2nd edn), Bristol: The Policy Press.

Campbell, C. (2002a) 'Conceptualisations and definitions of inclusive schooling', in C. Campbell (ed) *Developing inclusive schooling: Perspectives, policies and practices*, London: Institute of Education, pp 11-34.

Caplan, G. (1961) *A community approach to mental health*, London: Tavistock.

Caplan, G. (1964) *Principles of preventive psychiatry*, New York, NY: Basic Books.

Carr, S. (2008) *Personalisation: A rough guide*, London: Social Care Institute for Excellence.

Cleaver, H., Nicholson, D., Tarr, S. and Cleaver, D. (2007) *Child protection, domestic violence and parental substance misuse: Family experiences and effective practice*, London: Jessica Kingsley Publishers.

Clegg, A. and Megson, B. (1968) *Children in distress*, Harmondsworth: Penguin.

Clement, T. and Bigby, C. (2010) *Group homes for people with intellectual disabilities: Encouraging inclusion and participation*, London: Jessica Kingsley Publishers.

Cooper, D. (2000) *The death of the family*, New York, NY: Random House.

Coulshed, V. and Orme, J. (2006) *Social work practice: An introduction*, Basingstoke: Palgrave.

CPS (Crown Prosecution Service) (2009) *CPS violence against women crime report 2007-2008* (www.cps.gov.uk/publications/equality/vaw/index.html).

Cree, V. (2003) *Becoming a social worker*, London: Routledge.

CSCI (Commission for Social Care Inspection) (2007) *Risks and restraints: An exploration into the use of restraint in the care of older people*, London: CSCI.

Cunningham, J. and Cunningham, S. (2008) *Sociology and social work*, Exeter: Learning Matters.

Curtis Committee (1946) *Report of the Care of Children Committee*, Presented by the Secretary of State for the Home Department by the Minister of Health and the Minister of Education by the Command of His Majesty, London: HMSO.

Davies, M. (ed) (2000) *The Blackwell encyclopaedia of social work*, Oxford: Blackwell Publishers.

Davies, M. (ed) (2002) *The Blackwell companion to social work* (2nd edn), Oxford: Wiley-Blackwell.

DCSF (Department for Children, Schools and Families) (2008) *The Children's Plan: Building brighter futures*, London: The Stationery Office.

DCSF (2009) *Young runaways action plan*, London: The Stationery Office.

DfES (Department for Education and Skills) (2003) *Every Child Matters*, Green Paper, Cm 5860, London: The Stationery Office.

DfES and DH (2004) *National Service Framework for children, young people and maternity services*, London: The Stationery Office.

DCSF and DH (2009) *Building a Safe, Confident Future: The Final Report of the Social Work Taskforce*, London, DCSF

DH (Department of Health) (1998) *Modernising social services. Promoting independence, improving protection, raising standards*, Cm 4169, London: The Stationery Office.

DH (1999a) *National Service Framework for mental health*, London: DH.

DH (1999b) *Effective care co-ordination in mental health services – Modernising the care programme approach*, London: DH.

DH (1999c) *National Service Framework for mental health: Modern standards and service models*, London: DH.

DH (1999d) *Working together to safeguard children: A guide to inter-agency working to safeguard and promote the welfare of children*, London: The Stationery Office.

DH (2000) *Framework for the Assessment of Children in Need and their Families*, London: The Stationery Office.

DH (2001a) *Valuing People: A new strategy for learning disability in the twenty-first century*, Cm 5086, London: The Stationery Office.

DH (2001b) *National Service Framework for older people*, London: DH.

DH (2001c) *Single assessment framework*, London: DH.

DH (2002) *Women's mental health: Into the mainstream*, London: DH.

DH (2003) *Fair access to care services: Guidance on eligibility criteria for adult social care*, London: DH.

DH (2004a) *The ten essential shared capabilities. A framework for the whole of the mental health workforce*, London: DH.

DH (2004b) *A guide to receiving direct payments from your local council: A route to independent living*, London: DH.

DH (2005a) *Independence, well-being and choice: Our vision for the future of social care for adults in England*, Green Paper, London: DH.

DH (2005b) *Inpatients formally detained in hospitals under the Mental Health Act 1983 and other legislation, NHS trusts, care trusts and primary care trusts and independent hospitals: 2003-04*, London: DH.

DH (2005c) *New Ways of Working for psychiatry*, London: DH (www.newwaysofworking.org.uk).

DH (2006) *Our health, our care, our say: A new direction for community services*, Cm 6737, London: The Stationery Office.

DH (2007) *New Ways of Working for all*, London: DH (www.newwaysofworking.org.uk).

DH (2008a) *National end-of-life care strategy: Promoting high quality care for all adults at the end of life*, London: The Stationery Office.

DH (2008b) *Carers at the heart of 21st century families and communities: A caring system on your side, a life of your own*, London: DH.

DH (2009a) *Living well with dementia: A national dementia strategy*, London: DH.

DH (2009b) *Common assessment framework for adults: A consultation on proposals to improve information sharing around multi-disciplinary assessment and care plans*, London: DH.

DH and DETR (Department of the Environment, Transport and the Regions) (1999) *Better care, higher standards. A charter for long-term care*, London: The Stationery Office.

DH and Home Office (2000) *No secrets: Guidance on developing and implementing multi-agency policies and procedures to protect vulnerable adults from abuse*, London: The Stationery Office.

DHSSPS (Department of Health, Social Services and Public Safety) (2006) *The quality standards for health and social care*, Belfast: DHSSPS.

Doel, M. and Marsh, P. (1992) *Task-centred social work*, Aldershot: Ashgate.

Dominelli, L. (2004) *Social work: Theory and practice for a changing profession*, Cambridge: Polity Press.

Douglas, A. (2007) *Partnership working*, Abingdon, Oxon., Routledge.

Douglas, T. (1993) *A theory of groupwork practice*, Basingstoke: Macmillan.

Dryden, W. and Feltham, C. (1992) *Brief counselling: A practical guide for beginning practitioners*, Buckingham: Open University Press.

Duncombe, J. and Marsden, D. (1995) 'Women's "triple shift": paid employment, domestic labour and "emotion work"', *Sociology Review*, vol 4, no 4, April, pp 221-42.

Dustin, D. (2007) *The McDonaldization of social work*, Aldershot: Ashgate.

DWP (Department for Work and Pensions) (2004) *Delivering equality for disabled people*, Cm 6255, London: The Stationery Office.

Eborall, C. (2005) *The state of the social care workforce, 2004*, Skills Research and Intelligence 2nd Annual Report, April, Leeds: Skills for Care.

England, H. (1986) *Social work as art: Making sense for good practice*, London: Allen & Unwin.

Evans, C. and Carmichael, A. (2002) *A user-controlled best value review of direct payments*, York: Joseph Rowntree Foundation.

Fimister, G. (1986) *Welfare rights in social work*, Basingstoke: BASW/ Macmillan Education.

Fletcher-Campbell, F. and Archer, T. (2003) *Achievement at Key Stage 4 of young people in public care*, Slough: National Foundation for Educational Research.

Fook, J. and Gardner, F. (2007) *Practising critical reflection: A resource handbook*, Maidenhead: Open University Press.

Freire, P. (1986 [1972]) *Pedagogy of the oppressed*, Harmondsworth: Penguin.

Glasby, J. (2007) *Understanding health and social care*, Bristol: The Policy Press.

Glasby, J. and Dickinson, H. (2008) *Partnership working in health and social care*, Bristol: The Policy Press.

Glasby, J. and Lester, H. (2006) *Mental health: Policy and practice*, Basingstoke: Palgrave.

Goffman, E. (1968a) *Asylums: Essays on the social situation of mental patients and other inmates*, Harmondsworth: Penguin.

Goffman, E. (1968b) *Stigma: Notes on the management of spoiled identity*, Harmondsworth: Penguin.

Golan, N. (1978) *Treatment in crisis situations*, New York, NY: Free Press.

Golightley, M. (2008) *Social work and mental health* (3rd edn), Exeter: Learning Matters.

GSCC (General Social Care Council) (2002a) *Code of practice for social care workers*, London: GSCC.

GSCC (2002b) *Code of practice for employers of social care workers*, London: GSCC.

GSCC, CSCI (Commission for Social Care Inspection), SCIE (Social Care Institute for Excellence) and CWDC (Children's Workforce Development Council) (2008) *Social work at its best: The roles and tasks of social workers*, London: GSCC.

HM Government (2006) *Working together to safeguard children: A guide to inter-agency working to safeguard and promote the welfare of children*, London: The Stationery Office.

HM Government (2007) *Putting people first: A shared vision and commitment to the transformation of adult social care*, London: The Stationery Office.

HMSO (1969) *Report of the Committee of Inquiry into Allegations of Ill-treatment of Patients and other Irregularities at Ely Hospital, Cardiff*, Cmnd 3975, London: HMSO.

HMSO (1971) *Report of the Farleigh Hospital Committee of Inquiry*, Cmnd 4557, London: HMSO.

HMSO (1972) *Report of the Committee of Inquiry into Whittingham Hospital*, Cmnd 4861, London: HMSO.

HMSO (1978) *Report of the Committee into Normansfield Hospital*, Cmnd 7397, London: HMSO.

Hochschild, A.R. (1983) *The managed heart: Commercialisation of human feeling*, Berkeley, CA: University of California Press.

Horner, N. (2009) *What is social work: Contexts and perspectives* (3rd edn), Exeter: Learning Matters.

Hunter, M. (2009) 'We're sharing values now', *Community Care*, issue 1775, 18 June, pp 26-7.

IFSW (International Federation of Social Work) (2000) *Definition of social Work*, www.ifsw.org/p38000208.html

Institute of Community Cohesion (2008) *Understanding and appreciating Muslim cohesion: Towards better engagement and participation*, Coventry: Coventry University.

James, A. and James, A. (2004) *Constructing childhood: Theory, policy and social practice*, Basingstoke: Palgrave.

James, N. (1989) 'Emotional labour: skill and work in the regulation of feelings', *Sociological Review*, vol 37, pp 15-42.

Jones, K. (1972) *A history of the mental health services*, London: Routledge and Kegan Paul.

Kapoor, S. (2000) *Violence against women and girls*, Innocenti Digest no 6, June, Florence: UNICEF Innocenti Research Centre.

Kübler-Ross, E. (1982) *Living with death and dying*, London: Souvenir Press.

Laing, R.D. (1990) *The divided self: An existential study in sanity and madness*, Harmondsworth: Penguin.

Laming, H. (2003) *The Victoria Climbié Inquiry: Report of an Inquiry by Lord Laming*, Cm 5730, London: The Stationery Office.

Laming, H. (2009) *The protection of children in England: A progress report*, HC 330, London: The Stationery Office.

Ledwith, M. (2005) *Community development: A critical approach*, Bristol: The Policy Press.

Ledwith, M. and Springett, J. (2010) *Participatory practice: Community-based action for transformative change*, Bristol: The Policy Press.

Lindenfield, G. and Adams, R. (1984) *Problem-solving through self-help groups*, Ilkley: Self-Help Associates.

Lishman, J. (2007) *Handbook for practice learning in social work and social care* (2nd edn), London: Jessica Kingsley Publishers.

Lubovsky, V.I. (1974) 'Defectology: the science of handicapped children', *International Review of Education*, vol 20, no 3, September, pp 298-305.

Lymbery, M. (2007) *Social work with older people. Context, policy and practice*, London: Sage Publications.

McDonald, A., Postle, K. and Dawson, C. (2008) 'Barriers to retaining and using professional knowledge in local authority social work practice with adults in the UK', *British Journal of Social Work*, vol 38, pp 370-87.

McLeod, A. (2007) 'Whose agenda? Issues of power and relationship when listening to looked-after young people', *Child and Family Social Work*, vol 12, no 3, pp 278-86.

Magee, H., Parsons, S. and Askham, J. (2008) *Measuring dignity in care for older people: A research report for Help the Aged*, London: Help the Aged.

Maslow, A. (1943) 'A theory of human motivation', *Psychological Review*, vol 50, pp 370-96.

Maslow, A. (1987 [1968]) *Towards a psychology of being*, London: Harper Collins.

Matza, D. (1969) *Becoming deviant*, Englewood Cliffs, NJ: Prentice-Hall.

Mental Health Foundation (2008) *Recovery*, London: Mental Health Foundation (www.mentalhealth.org.uk/information/mental-health-a-z/recovery/).

Mezirow, J. 'Perspective transformation' *Adult Education*, 1978, 28: 100-10

Mind (2007) *Suicide factsheet*, London: Mind.

Morris, J. (1998) *Accessing human rights: Disabled children and the Children Act*, Ilford: Barnardo's.

O'Sullivan, T. (1999) *Decision Making in Social Work*, Basingstoke, Palgrave.

Parrott, L., Jacobs, G. and Roberts, D. (2008) *Stress and resilience factors in parents with mental health problems and their children*, Research briefing no 23, London: Social Care Institute for Excellence.

Parton, N. (2006) *Safeguarding childhood: Early intervention and surveillance in a late modern society*, Basingstoke: Palgrave.

Payne, M. (2005a) *The origins of social work: Continuity and change*, Basingstoke: Palgrave.

Payne, M. (2005b) *Modern social work theory* (3rd edn), Basingstoke: Palgrave.

Payne, M. (2006) *What is professional social work?* (2nd edn), Bristol: The Policy Press.

Payne, M. (2008) *Social care practice in context*, Basingstoke: Palgrave.

Phillips, J., Ray, M. and Marshall, M. (2006) *Social work with older people* (4th edn), Basingstoke: Palgrave.

Pike, S. and Forster, D. (1997) *Health promotion for all*, Edinburgh: Churchill Livingstone, pp 125-40.

PMSU (Prime Minister's Strategy Unit) (2007) *Building on progress: Public services*, HM Government Policy Review, London: The Stationery Office.

Preston-Shoot, M. (1987) *Effective groupwork*, Basingstoke: BASW/ Macmillan.

Ray, M., Pugh, R., Roberts, D. and Beech, B. (2008) *Mental health and social work*, Research briefing no 26, London: Social Care Institute for Excellence.

Reder, P. and Duncan, S. (2004) 'From Colwell to Climbié: inquiring into fatal child abuse', in N. Stanley and J. Manthorpe (eds) *The age of the inquiry: Learning and blaming in health and social care*, London: Routledge, pp 92-115.

Reid, W.J. (1963) *An experimental study of methods used in casework treatment*, New York, NY: School of Social Work, Columbia University.

Reid, W.J. and Epstein, L. (1972) *Task-centred casework*, New York, NY: Columbia University Press.

Reid, W.J. and Shyne, A.W. (1969) *Brief and extended casework*, New York, NY: Columbia University Press.

Repper, J. and Perskins, R. (2003) *Social inclusion and recovery. A model for mental health practice*, London: Balliere Tindall.

Ritchie, J. (1994) *Report of the Inquiry into the Care and Treatment of Christopher Clunis*, London: HMSO.

Robinson, P. (2008) *Working with young homeless people*, London: Jessica Kingsley Publishers.

Ryan, P. and Morgan, S. (eds) (2004) *Assertive outreach: A strengths approach to policy and practice*, Edinburgh: Churchill Livingstone.

Ryan, T. and Pritchard, J. (eds) (2004) *Good practice in adult mental health*, London: Jessica Kingsley Publishers.

Saegert, S. and Winkel, G. (1996) 'Paths to community empowerment: organising at home', *American Journal of Community Psychology*, vol 24, no 4, pp 517-50.

Sale, A.U. 'Hillingdon Social Work Team eases children into UK life' *Community Care*, 22 Aug 2008 pp. 20-1.

Saleeby, D. (2002) *The strengths perspective in social work practice* (3rd edn), New York, NY: Allyn and Bacon.

Scopulus (2008) *Survey of learning disability*, London: Mencap.

Scottish Executive (2002) *Guidance on single shared assessment of community care needs*, Edinburgh: The Stationery Office.

Scottish Executive (2004) *Changing lives: Report of the 21st century social work review*, Edinburgh: Scottish Executive.

Scottish Executive (2006) *Changing lives implementation plan*, Edinburgh: Scottish Executive.

Scottish Government (2009) *The evidence base for third sector policy in Scotland: A review of selected recent publications* (www.scotland.gov.uk/ Publications/2009/10/16155044/3).

Sedgwick, P. (1982) *Psycho politics*, London: Pluto Press.

Seebohm Report (1968) *Report of the Committee on Local Authority and Allied Personal Social Services*, Cmnd 3703, London, HMSO.

Shakespeare, T. (2006) *Disability rights and wrongs*, London: Routledge.

Social Exclusion Task Force, (2007) *Reaching out: Think family. Analysis and themes from the Families At Risk Review*, London: Cabinet Office.

Social Work Task Force (2009a) *Facing up to the task: The interim report of the Social Work Task Force: July 2009*, London: DCSF (http://publications. dcsf.gov.uk/).

Social Work Task Force (2009b) *Building a safe, confident future: The final report of the Social Work Task Force: November 2009*, London: DCSF (http://publications.dcsf.gov.uk/).

Sontag, S. (1966) *Against interpretation and other essays*, New York: Farr, Straus and Girou.

Stanton, A. (1990) 'Empowerment of staff: a prerequisite for the empowerment of users', in P. Carter, T. Jeffs and M. Smith (eds) *Social work and social welfare yearbook 2*, Buckingham: Open University Press, pp 122-33.

Stedman Jones, G. (1971) *Outcast London: A study in the relationship between classes in Victorian society*, Harmondsworth: Penguin.

Stepney, P. and Popple, K. (2008) *Social work and the community: A critical context for practice*, Basingstoke: Palgrave.

Sullivan, M.P. (2008) 'Social workers in community care practice: ideologies and interactions with older people', *British Journal of Social Work*, May, pp 1-20.

Sure Start Unit (2002) *Birth to three matters: A framework to support children in their earliest years*, London: Department for Education and Skills.

Szasz, T.S. (1970) *The manufacture of madness*, New York, NY: Harper and Row.

Szasz, T.S. (1990) *Insanity: The idea and its consequences*, New York, NY: Wiley.

Taylor, A. (2009) 'Multiple choice', *Community Care*, 12 March, issue 1761, pp 28-9.

Terry, P. (1997) *Counselling the elderly and their carers*, Basingstoke: Macmillan.

Thompson, N. (2000) *Understanding social work: Preparing for practice*, Basingstoke: Palgrave.

Thompson, N. (2001) *Anti-discriminatory practice*, Basingstoke: Palgrave.

Thornicroft, G. and Kassam, A. (2008) *Mental Health Research Network (MHRN): Stigma and Discrimination Research Group. Six-month report*, London: Institute of Psychiatry.

Topss (Training Organisation for the Personal Social Services) UK Partnership (2004) *National Occupational Standards for social workers*, Leeds: Topss (www.skillsforcare.org.uk).

Tracy, G.S. and Gussow, Z. (1976) 'Self-help groups: a grassroots response to a need for services' *Journal of Applied Behavioural Science*, 12, Part 3: 381-96.

Travis, A. (2009) 'Classroom drive to curb violence in relationships', *Society Guardian*, 25 November (www.guardian.co.uk/society/2009/nov/25/violence-prevention-classes).

Turner, C. (2003) *Are you listening? What disabled children and young people in Wales think about the services they use*, Cardiff: Welsh Assembly Government.

Twelvetrees, A. (2008) *Community work* (4th edn), Basingstoke: Palgrave.

UN (United Nations) (1948) *Universal Declaration of Human Rights*, Geneva: UN.

UN (1993) *UN Declaration on the Elimination of Violence Against Women*, Geneva: UN.

UN (2006) *Rights of the child: Report of the independent expert for the United Nations study on violence against children*, Geneva: UN (www.violencestudy.org/IMG/pdf/English/pdf).

WAG (Welsh Assembly Government) (2004a) *Safeguarding children. Working together under the Children Act 2004*, Cardiff: WAG.

WAG (2004b) *Children and young people: Rights to action*, Cardiff: WAG.

Walker, A., O'Brien, M., Traynore, J., Goddards, E. and Foster, K. (2002) *Living in Britain: Results from the 2001 General Household Survey*, London: Office for National Statistics.

Ward, D. (2009) 'Groupwork', in R. Adams, L. Dominelli and M. Payne (eds) *Critical practice in social work*, Basingstoke: Palgrave, pp 114-24.

Whitaker, D.S. (1985) *Using groups to help people*, London: Tavistock/Routledge.

Williams, C. (2008) 'Walking the social work beat', *Community Care*, issue 1722, 15 May, pp 20-1.

Windfuhr, K., While, D., Hunt, I., Turnbull, P., Lowe, R., Burns, J., Swinson, N., Shaw, J., Appleby, L. and Kapur, N. (2008) 'National confidential inquiry into suicide and homicide by people with mental illness: suicide in juveniles and adolescents in the United Kingdom', *Journal of Child Psychology and Psychiatry*, vol 49, no 11, pp 1157-67.

Wolfensberger, W. (1972) *The principle of normalisation in human services*, Toronto: National Institute on Mental Retardation.

Wolfensberger, W. (1982) 'Social role valorisation: a proposed new term for the principle of normalisation', *Mental Retardation*, vol 21, no 6, pp 234-9.

There are two main levels of the structure for the qualifying and post-qualifying education and training of social workers:

- initial qualifying education and training on a higher education course leading to a degree qualification (dealt with in Chapter Two);
- engaging in continuing professional development after qualification.

At the point of qualification, the practitioner demonstrates sufficient expertise to be granted registration by the General Social Care Council (GSCC) or its equivalent bodies in Wales, Scotland and Northern Ireland, as a social care worker, thus acquiring the legal right to use the title of social worker and to practise social work.

The point of qualification marks not only the start of a career but also an early stage in a commitment to continuing professional development. This is expected of the practitioner, in order that updating takes place in line with changing legislation and agency expectations, as well as the development of greater expertise.

The Social Work Task Force (2009b) proposes reforms to the structure of social work education, with changes in the basic and subsequent courses of qualification, clearer roles and career structure for social workers and an improved system of continuing professional development.

A new, assessed year as an employed social worker will be the final stage of the process of initial qualification, leading to becoming a licensed, practising social worker.

Continuing professional development

The Social Work Task Force (2009b) envisages that high quality continuing professional development will form the basis for the newly qualified social worker developing expertise, fresh knowledge and understanding and confidence as a practitioner. Post-qualification courses will move towards provision of a Masters in Social Work Practice.

Reregistration of social workers is required every three years and the Social Work Task Force (2009b) recommends that this process is made more rigorous and demanding. The proposed career structure of social workers, in the light of the recommendations of the Social Work Task Force, will look as follows (Figure A.1):

Figure A.1: Proposed career structure of social workers

Advanced professional/Practice educator/Social work manager

Senior licensed social worker   following post-qualifying programme

Licensed social worker   following successful assessment

Probationary social worker   assessed first year in employment

Undergraduate degree qualification   following successful graduation

Social work student   undergraduate level

The introduction of a nationally recognised career structure for social workers, assuming the Social Work Task Force recommendations are implemented, will set enhanced standards not only for social workers but also for their employers. Career progression involves the practitioner moving on to a post-qualifying programme and, perhaps, selecting to continue into advanced practice, or into practice education. Another practitioner would, perhaps, specialise in social work management. Further specialist standards are identified by the Social Work Task Force in child protection, mental health and safeguarding. There is the prospect, if this integrated structure for continuing professional development is implemented over the next few years by employers, colleges and universities, that social workers will be rewarded in terms of enhanced status and pay, perhaps regardless of whether they choose to stay in practice at a more advanced level, move into practice education or become social work managers.

Registration bodies

England
General Social Care Council (GSCC): www.gscc.org.uk

Wales
Care Council for Wales: www.ccwales.org.uk

Scotland
Scottish Social Services Council (SSSC): www.sssc.uk.com

Northern Ireland
Northern Ireland Social Care Council (NISCC): www.niscc.info

British Association of Social Workers (BASW): www.basw.co.uk

index

Note: the letters f and t following page numbers refer to figures and tables.

A

accountabilities 79–80, 81
ADHD 119–20
adult care trusts 76
adults and health-related services
  adult social care 126–7
  alcohol problems 144
  assessment processes 135
  care services, payment for 127, 129
  carers 126, 136–8
  community care 138–9
  direct payments 126–7
  drug problems 144
  end-of-life strategy 138
  health inequalities 127–8
  health promotion 128–9
  hospital-based social work 141–2
  integrated services 15
  legal basis for practice 135, 136t
  mental capacity 142–3
  needs 139, 140t
  personalisation 126–7, 131–2, 133–6,
    143–4, 145–6
  practice 144–6
    approaches to 142–3
    settings for 141–2
  preventive health services 129
  rights of adults 136t
  see also older people
advocacy work 21–2, 121, 122
ageing society 150, 151–2
ageism 156
alcohol problems 112, 113, 144
Alzheimer's disease 161, 162
anorexia 160
anorexia nervosa 160–1
anti-discriminatory strategies 156
approved mental health professionals
  (AMHPs) 190, 192–3
approved social workers (ASWs) 190
asylum seekers 113–14
attention-deficit hyperactivity disorder
  (ADHD) 119–20

B

Baby Peter 66, 98
Barnes, C. 175
Biestek, F.P. 41
Bigby, C. 179
biography 52–8
Bradshaw, J. 13, 91
Brandon, D. 21, 23–4, 25
brief therapy 19
British Association of Social Workers
  (BASW) 42
bulimia 160
Bulter, I. 90

C

Campbell, C. 169
Caplin, G. 19
care, children in 110–11
care homes 127
Care Quality Commission (CQC) 70
care services, payment for 127, 129
Care Standards Act (2000) 127
career structure, proposed 218–19
carers 126, 136–8, 159, 164–5, 188–9
Carers (Recognition and Services) Act
  (1995) 159
Carers and Disabled Children Act (2000)
  159
Carers UK 138
Carr, S. 131–2
change work 18, 20–1
Charity Organisation Society (COS) 6–7
child abuse 95–6, 98, 104–5
child and adolescent mental health 190,
  194, 195
Child and Adolescent Mental Health
  Services (CAMHS) 190, 194
Child Protection Conference 107
child protection services, shortcomings 67
childhood as social construction 92–3

Children Act (1989) 15–16, 73–4, 95–7, 104, 106
Children Act (2004) 67, 76, 95, 99–100
children and families 89–91
  alcohol problems 112, 113
  asylum seekers 113–14
  children, different views of 92–3
  children in care 110–11
  death and bereavement, helping children to deal with 112
  disabled children, preferences 110
  diversity 100
  domestic violence 113, 115
  drug problems 112–13
  family structures 91–2
  health and well-being 112
  homelessness 118
  integrated services 15
  intervention 96, 100, 101, 106, 114–15
  investigatory social work 105
  legal basis for practice 95–100
  local authority services 94–5
  'no order' principle 107
  obesity 112
  parenting 115–17
  policy 94–5
  poverty and social exclusion 115–17
  practice
    approaches to 101–2
    child-centred practice 102, 103f
    core assessment 107–9
    implementation 110–11
    initial assessment 107
    integrated children's system 104
    key stages 104
    planning services 109–10
    settings for 101–2
  prevention 100–1
  refugees 113–14
  risk 100–1
  safeguarding children 98, 117–18
  social workers in schools 119
  special needs 119–21
  Sure Start local programmes (SSLPs) 101–2
Children and Family Court Advisory and Support Service (CAFCASS) 118
Children Leaving Care Act (2000) 111
The Children's Plan (2008) 15
children's commissioner 83
children's rights 94, 121–2
children's services 89
children's trusts 76
chronic illness 128
citizen advocacy 21
Cleaver, H. 144
Clement, T. 179

Climbié, Victoria 98
code of ethical practice 42, 82
cognitive behavioural therapy 19, 196
collective advocacy 21
Commission for Patient and Public Involvement in Health (CPPIH) 126
Commission for Social Care Inspection (CSCI) 70
commodification 80–1
communities, work with 208–13
  approaches to 210–11
  community capacity building 213
  community development 208
  community profiling 213
  contexts of 209–10
  definition 208–9
  networking 212
  practice 211–13
Community Care (Direct Payments) Act (1996) 76
community care services 130, 138–9
Community Service Volunteers (CSV) 34
complaints procedures 83, 127
conscientisation 204–5
consciousness raising 204, 206
Continuing Professional Development (CPD) 218
counselling 19, 196
courts 73–5
CRB check 32, 41
Cree, V. 5
crisis intervention 19
critically reflective practice 59–60, 62f

D

death
  and end-of-life care 138, 141–2
  helping children deal with 112
dementia 160, 161–3
devolution 75
dignity in care 156–7
direct payments 76–7, 126–7, 130–1
disability 167
Disability Discrimination Act (1995) 173
Disability Discrimination Act (2006) 173
disability movement 170
Disability Rights Movement 186
disabled people 167–8
  discrimination 168, 170, 173
  group care 179
  inclusiveness 159
  legal basis for practice 172–3
  models of disability 174–7
  person-centred planning 170–1
  policy changes 168–70

practice 177–80
  approaches to 174–7
  key issues 179
  settings for 173–4
  self-advocacy 177–8
disablism 173
discretion 81
discrimination 84, 168, 170, 173
diversity among people 83, 84
domestic violence 113, 115
domiciliary care 127, 154–5
Douglas, A. 69
Drakeford, M. 90
drug therapy 196
drugs misuse 112–13
Duncombe, J. 20, 21
Dustin, D. 81

E

eating disorders 160–1
Eborall, C. 4, 10
education in social work *see* qualifying
  social work programme
emotion work 20–1
end-of-life care 138, 141–2, 149–50
Equality Act (2006) 173
ethical principles 42, 43, 45, 82
Europe, social work 9
European Convention on Human Rights
  (ECHR) (1950) 75
European legislation 75
Every Child Matters Green Paper (2003)
  94, 98

F

Fair access to care services (2003) 156
families *see* children and families
family therapy 19, 196
Fimister, G. 22
Freire, P. 204–5

G

gender inequality 91–2
General Social Care Council (GSCC) 41,
  42, 217
Goffman, E. 184
Golan, N. 19
group work 203–8
  approaches to 206
  consciousness-raising 204
  definition 205–6
  group care settings 206

group's 'life' stages 207
  practising group work 207–8
  running a group 207–8
  self-help groups 206, 207
GSCC 41, 42, 217
Gussow, Z. 206

H

Health and Social Care (Community
  Health Standards) Act (2003) 70
health and social services 125
  carers 136–7
  community care 138–9
  contracting services 130, 131t
  end-of-life care strategy 138
  health promotion 128–9
  modernisation 128–33
  personalisation 133–6
  see also adults and health-related
    services
health inequalities 127–8
Healthcare Commission (HCC) 70
Hochschild, A.R. 20
home care 127, 154–5
Home Life Project 157
homelessness 118
homosexuality 188
hospital-based social work 141–2
Human Givens strategy 196
Human Rights Act (1998) 75

I

impairment 167
independent sector 68–9
individual budgets 127, 143, 144, 145
inequalities 91–2, 127–8, 150–1
informal carers 136–7
informed consent 163
inquiry reports 89–90
intervention work 18, 25, 26f
investigatory social work 105

J

James, N. 20
Jordan, B. 23–4, 25

K

Kapoor, S. 91–2

L

Laming, Lord 98
laws 72–3
learning disability 168
Ledwith, M. 51
legal basis for services 76–7, 78t
legal system 72–5
  courts 73–5
  European legislation 75
  laws 72–3
  tribunals 74
  UK legislation 75
legislation 76–7, 78t
life history work 19–20
Lishman, J. 59
local authorities 70, 76–7
  adult care services 132–3, 134f
  children's services 94–5
Local Authority Social Services Act (1970) 76, 153
local involvement networks (LINks) 126

M

managerialism 80–1
Marsden, D. 20, 21
Maslow, A. 12–13, 14
mental capacity 154
Mental Capacity Act (2005) 142–3, 154, 164, 188
Mental Health Act (1983) 143, 188, 189, 199, 200
Mental Health Act (2007) 143, 188
mental health and illness 183–4, 189
  carers 188–9
  child and adolescent mental health 194, 195
  community care 193–4
  historical perspective 185
  legal basis for practice 188–90
  mental health problems 184–5
  models of mental health 186–8
  practice 197–201
    approaches to 194–7
    assertive community treatment 198
    assertive outreach 198
    crisis resolution 198
    discharge from hospital 200
    holistic approach 197
    mental hospital, admission and discharge 199–200
    psychiatric intensive care 199
    recovery approaches 197–8
    risk management 200–1
    sectioning 199
    service-user participation 201

  settings for 193–4
  practice shortcomings 185–6
  self-help groups 187–8
  young carers 189
Mental Health Foundation 198
mental health work
  dual diagnosis 192
  national standards 189–90
  New Ways of Working 191–2
  post-qualifying practice 192–3
  social workers' roles 190–1
  see also mental health and illness
mental hospital, admittance and discharge 199–200
Mezirow, J. 50
Mind 184, 196

N

National Assistance Act (1948) 153, 154, 172
National Care Standards Commission 127
National Occupational Standards (NOS) 36, 42–3, 44t
National Service Framework for older people (2001) 155, 156, 158
national standards
  for mental health work 189–90
  for older people's services 153–4
National Survivor User Network 187
National Treatment Agency for Substance Misuse (NTA) 113
needs
  community care, assessment of 139, 140t
  definition 12–13
  holistic approaches to 14–15
  Maslow's pyramid of 14
  and personalisation 16–17
  relative not absolute 13
  and rights, tension between 15–16
networking 20, 212
New Ways of Working 191–2
NHS and Community Care Act (1990) 76, 77, 130, 138–9
Northern Ireland 65–6, 70, 71

O

obesity 112
Ofsted 70, 71
older people 149–50
  care homes 157–8
  carers 164–5
  dignity in care 156–7
  home care 154–5
  inequalities 150–1

intermediate care 155
legal basis for practice 152–3
mental capacity 154
national standards for services 153–4
personal care 156
personalisation 155
practice
  care planning 159
  dementia 161–3
  eating disorders 160–1
  integrated practice 158
  intervention 159
  key issues 164–5
  monitoring 159
  networking 159
  safeguarding older people 160
  single assessment 158–9
  transitions 163
residential care 154, 155
risk assessment 159
social care 156
see also adults and health-related
  services
organisation of social work 65–72
  changes, 21st century 66–7
  partnership working 67–9
  quality assurance 71
  regulation of standards 71
O'Sullivan, T. 61

P

palliative care 141, 149–50
partnership working 67–9
Pedagogy of the oppressed (Freire) 204
peer advocacy 21
people's needs *see* needs
personal care 156
personal statements 51–8
personalisation 16–17, 126–7, 131–2,
  133–6, 143–4, 145–6
Popple, K. 208
Princess Royal Trust for Carers 138
principles of social work 41–2, 43t
private sector 68–9, 130
professional advocacy 21–2
professional qualifications *see* qualifying
  social work programme
professionalism 49–50
psychiatric treatment 187
psychotherapy 19

Q

qualifying social work programme
  age of applicants 33–4
application 32–4, 48–9, 51–2
assessment 39, 40f, 41f, 43
critically reflective practice 59–60, 62f
expertise 58, 59f
knowledge and understanding 35
learning process 58–60, 62f
outline of 34–5
personal statement 51–8
practice education 35–9, 59
  evaluation 39, 40
  observed practice 37–9
  placement report 37
  reflection 37
reflective diary 50
research 63
standards of attainment 41f
supervision 59, 60–2

R

Recovery International 198
reflexivity 50
refugees 113–14
registration 40–1, 217
regulation 40–1, 71
rights
  of adults 136t
  of children 94, 121–2
  and needs, tension between 15–16
Robinson, P. 118

S

Saegert, S. 210
safeguarding children 98, 117–18
safeguarding older people 160
Safeguarding Vulnerable Groups Act (2006)
  160
Saleeby, D. 143
'sceptical stance' 105, 121
schools, social workers in 119
Scotland
  direct payments 76–7
  healthcare 127, 129
  social work organisation 65, 66, 67, 70–1
Sedgwick, P. 187
self-help groups 187–8, 206, 207
Shakespeare, T. 175–6
single assessment 158–9
social care 3
Social Care Register 31–2
social care services 3–5
social exclusion 115–16
social inequalities 127–8, 150–1
social security 3
social services 3–4

social work 3
  definition 5
  key features of 10–11
  nature of 5–6, 8–9
  organisation of 65–72
    changes, 21st century 66–7
    partnership working 67–9
    quality assurance 71
    regulation of standards 71
  origins of 6–7
  principles of 41–2, 43t
  tensions in 25, 26f
  themes of 8f
  values of 42, 43t, 45
Social Work Task Force 31, 67, 217, 218
social workers
  qualities of 23–4
  roles of 17–22
    advocacy work 21–2
    change work 18, 20–1
    counselling 19
    crisis intervention 19
    emotion work 20–1
    intervention work 18
    networking 20
    task-centred work 18–19
    tensions in 25, 26t
    therapy 19–20
  workforce 10
special needs, children with 119–21
Springett, J. 51
Stanton, A. 203
statutes 81–2
Stepney, P. 208
substance misuse 112–13
suicide 185, 194
Sure Start local programmes (SSLPs)
    101–2
Survivors Speak Out 187
Szasz, T.S. 187

T

task-centred work 18–19
Terry, P. 19
therapy 19–20
third sector 69–71
Tracy, G.S. 206
training see qualifying social work
    programme
transformative learning 50–1
tribunals 74, 83
Twelvetrees, A. 209, 210

U

UN Convention on the Rights of the Child
    (UNCRC) 15, 94
Universal Declaration of Human Rights (UN)
    15

V

values 42, 43t, 45
Valuing People White Paper (2001) 168–9,
    170
violence 91–2, 98, 113, 115
voluntary sector 68–9, 70, 130
voluntary work 34

W

Wales
  children's rights 94
  healthcare 127, 129
  social work organisation 65, 67, 70, 71
Winkel, G. 210
Wolfensberger, W. 175
women, violence against 91–2
world, differences in social work 9

Y

young carers 137–8, 189
young people see children and families